To My "Greatest" Great A, Enjoy the Verna AKA Bella

# Closing Chapter

# Closing Chapter

Memoir of a Daughter's Grief

Bella

iUniverse

**CLOSING CHAPTER**
**MEMOIR OF A DAUGHTER'S GRIEF**

Copyright © 2016 Bella.

All rights reserved. No part of this book may be used or reproduced by any means, graphic, electronic, or mechanical, including photocopying, recording, taping or by any information storage retrieval system without the written permission of the author except in the case of brief quotations embodied in critical articles and reviews.

iUniverse books may be ordered through booksellers or by contacting:

iUniverse
1663 Liberty Drive
Bloomington, IN 47403
www.iuniverse.com
1-800-Authors (1-800-288-4677)

Because of the dynamic nature of the Internet, any web addresses or links contained in this book may have changed since publication and may no longer be valid. The views expressed in this work are solely those of the author and do not necessarily reflect the views of the publisher, and the publisher hereby disclaims any responsibility for them.

Any people depicted in stock imagery provided by Thinkstock are models, and such images are being used for illustrative purposes only.
Certain stock imagery © Thinkstock.

ISBN: 978-1-4917-8900-1 (sc)
ISBN: 978-1-4917-8897-4 (e)

Library of Congress Control Number: 2016901640

Print information available on the last page.

iUniverse rev. date: 03/10/2016

Chapter One

# Mama's Life

Some of us get to rehearse. Others are somewhat prepared. Some are not prepared at all. But with all the preparations in the world, the time comes, and death has a starring role. We are never ready. Mama's life played out against the backdrop of my childhood.

The phone woke me from a deep sleep. "Hello?"

"Bella," the voice said between sobs, "Mama's gone."

"What?" I looked at the time; it was 3:37 a.m. eastern time. The dawn's light was dissolving the darkness in the room. "Cicely, what are you saying?" I knew what she had said. I wanted her to say it again.

"Mama died this morning."

I took in a deep breath before I spoke. "She died?" I asked. I was answering with a question.

"Bell, Bell, Mama's gone. She's gone!"

I couldn't speak. Bell was short for Bella. I was the second oldest. What was set before me was an unwelcome occurrence; death had set the stage for the final call. Mama had taken her last bow. The curtain fell for the last time. What legacy would Mama leave?

Cicely, my youngest sister, was still living at home. Mama had six children. Maya was the oldest, and I was the middle daughter. Mama had her sons last. We called Edward "Eddie."

We called Philip "Lip." And Anthony was called "Tony." I didn't have any idea how they felt. I didn't know how I felt. I didn't break down and cry. I just held the phone after Cicely had hung up. Sitting on the side of the bed, covered in the half-dark bedroom, I sat there next to the window. I was thinking about the day the city workers woke me, cutting down the tree that had covered the window for twenty years. I could almost reach out and touch the leaves on the branches.

Cicely said Mama passed sometime between eleven at night and three in the morning. I heard Cicely but was not ready for what she was telling me. Are you supposed to be ready? Mama had been sick for a while. I needed time. Time was everything. I hoped Mama knew that I had loved her. I felt at that moment like a channel for the living. I wanted to pour all of what I knew onto my mama and bring her back to fix what was wrong with the family.

Mama had been confined to the Edgewood Nursing Home by my sister Cicely with the help of Aunt Tamar. I was planning to see Mama for Christmas. I went home when she was admitted to the nursing home. Neither Cicely nor Aunt Tamar was there. I had last seen her in October. I would go home every three months to visit Mama at the Edgewood Nursing Home. I planned to stay for two weeks, but I could never make the two weeks. Mama and I would fight throughout my visit. Something I'd said or done would set her off. I don't know why we fought.

It mattered how much of this I was responsible for. Sometimes I would cut my visits short and leave without a word. I needed to find a way to my peace. Mama and I needed to heal the wounds. I felt Mama turning from me. She had told me, of all her kids, she knew I loved her least. What did that mean? Now I could understand it. How was I to love her? Was it something I had to learn? It bothered me for many years. My heart hurt as I remembered those words spoken years before.

I was thirteen and coming into my own, exploring who I was in this large family, with Mama's fifteen sisters and brothers. There was Grandmama and Grandpapa. It was a village.

My mother's name was Rachel Thurston. There were fifteen sisters and brothers. I grew up where whopping was the order of the day. Getting a whopping was less hurtful than the words Mama spoke. Mama could say mean-spirited words with charm. Mama always smiled when hurting your feelings.

Mama was a very strong-willed woman. Mama got noticed. She was very beautiful. I was changed by those words spoken that day. I wouldn't let Mama see me cry after that. I remember Mama giving me a whopping. I would shout, "Mama! Mama!" for the whole neighborhood to hear.

Mama hated it when anyone screamed. "Why do you always act like I'm killing you?" Mama shouted back. I would run downstairs crying to Grandmama. I needed her to tell me that this was not all right.

Grandpapa and Grandmama lived downstairs; Mama and her six children lived upstairs. "Why does my mama think that I don't love her, Grandmama?" I ran into her arms, crying and saying, "I do love my mama." But Mama always whooped me for things Cicely did.

Grandmama listened. She looked long and deep into my eyes, not blinking. Grandmama said, "You are her different child, baby." That was all she said. She rubbed the tears from my eyes and told me to go blow my nose. Grandmama took her needle and started to thread it. I knew that day that I would do my best never to cry or let my emotions control my feelings. I knew Mama didn't want me. I felt her energy. But I was born, and I was here.

On one of my many visits to the nursing home, we had one of our fights. I left tasting the salty tears running down my face. I cried as I recalled Grandmama's words: "You're just different, honey." Walking to the bus stop, I couldn't remember what the conversation was about, only that I had lost control of my emotions, which gave way to this river of tears. Mama could easily hurt me, but I would never let her see me cry. I knew Mama was bothered that her words never bothered me, but how wrong she had been. But Mama didn't know my real pain. What she said affected me and had affected me all my life, more than she could know. On this visit, Mama thought I had packed my bags again and left for home without good-byes. Had the nurse called New York the next day? I hadn't left; I was still in New Orleans. I stayed to face whatever past hurts, pains, or scares would be inflicted upon me. The next day I showed up and began to heal. "You will not receive another chance," the voice inside my head said. "'This time will be your last visit." I knew this feeling. I had had this voice with me for as long as I could remember.

I visited Mama that morning, and she was surprised to see me walk into her room. I leaned over and kissed her on the lips, as I always did, and whispered, "Mama, I know I was a difficult child, and I want and need you to forgive me."

Mama looked at me and gave me that smile she gave when she was going to hurt your feelings. "You know you hurt me deeply, but I can forgive you for not loving me like you loved your daddy."

I was happy that I had stayed. I found the answer to why she felt the way she did all these years. My healing process had begun. I would forever trust this feeling. Mama had started to look much better than she had in a long time.

Mama had come a long way. It had been more than two years that she had been lying in the nursing home bed, refusing to get up. From the beginning I had watched my mama refuse the physical therapy. Mama had to use the bedpan, and she hated that thing. It was too small. Mama was standing when she first got there, but now she wouldn't get out of bed, not even to sit in the chair. She was becoming difficult as the days turned into months and the months became years. I wondered why she would want to live out her last days in this state. This was not the strong and able woman who'd caught the bus every day to work for thirty-four years to raise six children. Mama had helped her mother raise her other sisters and brothers, as well.

I now had come to a chapter that was closing. I accepted what I had come to know. Family was somehow lost to me.

Rachel's children were no longer connected—not like Mama had been with her siblings. We were very close as children. But this was not about who we were. It was truly about who we had become. Holding my breath, I did not know how to take it all in. *Breathe.* I felt myself come back to the present. My mother was no longer in the physical world. Her life opened before me in different colors. Flashes of time measured Mama's soul and released her personality. My mama energy had moved beyond time and space. I had long since planned what I would say at Mama's funeral when she died. I would let them all know how I felt.

After Mama retired, she found out she had influenza and got on oxygen. I don't think I took Mama's illness seriously until we went on the cruise. Mama had always wanted to go to Jamaica, but the cruise was overbooked. Mama's second choice was the Bahamas. Mama couldn't talk about the cruise enough. It excited Mama to let people know her daughter would be taking her. Travel became impossible for Mama after our cruise. She stayed in now, and we stayed on the phone. Our relationship changed, but we always disagreed.

Mama attended church and family functions if she got a ride. Mama was the one to plan most of the family events. The phone was the only outlet Mama used well. Cousin Briana, Aunt Tamar's daughter, had gotten Mama a computer, but she didn't have an interest in it other than playing spades. Mama loved playing cards.

Bid whist, the card game, had been the reason for family gatherings every Friday night. Mama and her sisters and brothers would get together to fry fish and play cards. Every Friday the games would end with a fight. Few visits from her sisters and brothers became the highlight of the conversation on Fridays. After a while Mama would often comment about those who didn't come by because of their busy lives. I longed for Mama to have some kind of peace, longing for the old days.

My visits at home were not always the most enjoyable, even before Mama went into the nursing home. We never could see eye to eye on anything; words or a certain look often got in our way. Mama and I just never lasted very long on any one topic. It was always because I said so or because she had read it in the paper. My mama read the paper from front to back. Mama kept week-old papers on the kitchen table, on kitchen chairs, and on the kitchen floor next to the corner where she sat an arm's length from the wall phone.

Mama missed her sisters and brothers needing her. Mama had much patience, but where were they now? And when I did see them at Mama's house, Cicely created this energy that made them feel uncomfortable. Cicely became the moving force that influenced Mama after Cicely and her youngest son had moved in.

Life finally was becoming comfortable for Mama. She had been retired for five years when she became sick. Being confined to the house was very aggravating to Mama, so the visits from family were joyful. Mama said her house was starting to feel like a day care with Cicely's grandchildren. Cicely had been the reason Mama's sisters and brothers stopped visiting. Cicely had moved back home. They also said they didn't really understand her or her behavior toward their sister Rachel. They didn't know how to address the situation. Many of them expressed that sentiment. But they did not give her a measure of concern, because Cicely, who, without Mama's knowledge, would disrespect everyone who often visited. I understood how Cicely could make one feel. Over time how many trips to the supermarket did they offer? "They went where they know I don't drive," Mama said with a tone of jealousy, because Mama never learned how to drive. Why had they not visited their sister who had been there for them during their many storms of life? I recall many times my mama was there for them. There were too many to count. I was there through all their troubles. They were part of my childhood. I grew up with my aunts.

While Mama was confined to the nursing home, her sisters and brothers abandoned her. Where was their support? Those who I thought mattered never came to visit as much as they

*Closing Chapter*

should have. My sisters, Cicely and Maya, were just thirty minutes away. Maya visited only twice in two years. I think none of us visited enough. What had gone wrong, given all that Mama had done? What is that saying? *If one can care for six, how is it six cannot care for one?*

When the phone would ring, Mama would get up and start down the long hallway to the kitchen, turn on the lights, and put on a pot of coffee. Because in those wee hours of the night lying in bed hearing the knock at the door. Waken from my sleep because one of Mama's sisters or brothers had no place to go, because Grandpapa had rules and wouldn't let them in downstairs. Mama siblings always knew her door was never closed

After Mama went to the nursing home, most of her siblings got their lives together. Was it because they now had a sister who was old and sickly and they had nowhere to turn but to themselves? For the most part they were all doing quite well. Souls that achieve peace from sorrow have the capability to learn love. Some memories are meant to fade as we learn life expressions. I had just visited Mama in October. I had my last performance. Death was there. It had settled over Mama's life, set the stage, measured the worth, and played the role. Rachel had been a good mother, a good sister, and a loving daughter. I know now that it was never about the material gains but spiritual connections that had come full circle. I have been blessed. I know now the struggle Mama had raising six children, but I also know its worth. Some mothers live their unfulfilled dreams, wishes, and desires through their children. I know now Mama gave hers up. I wanted to be there for Mama. I wanted to give her her wishes and desires, like Mama's seventieth birthday party, a wish she said she always wanted. Mama's papa and her mama had never given my mama or her sisters or brothers a birthday party. It was my delight to do this! I have learned to turn inward when disturbance arises. The soft kindness of Mama's voice and gentleness of her tone brought harmony to my soul. My soul was now consumed with a knowing.

The fruits of my life were these seeds that had been planted, and the roots ran deep. Mama was living water that brought blooms after a storm. Did my mother influence me or control me in subtle ways? Yes. But never would I allow her to dominate me. I could have my freedom. I was taking a journey back to myself and the peace that surpasses one's being. Looking inward, I had found my source—a loving being whom I could draw to me in joy, sorrow, or distress.

My biological father didn't abandon me; he was my world. Daddy tried many times to live with Mama and make us a family, but it was never to be. Mama's papa always found the excuse: Daddy was too old. Mama loved having a good time, and Daddy loved his good time too. Not much was secret in my childhood.

There was always a sense of shame around the rapes. Mama, Cicely, and I had this horrible experience. I wondered most of my life if Mama was hiding our shame or hiding her shame. I had an intense bond with my sister Cicely because of what had happened to us. I always meditated on our well-being. It's funny what we think about when we sit in our pain. I know that Mama would have given her life for any of us. She was the glue that held the entire family together. Even Aunt Tamar had confessed that Mama was the matriarch after she sold the house on Esplanade Avenue. I remembered that house well. The family moved to Esplanade Avenue when I was four years old. Mama had just had Cicely. Most people who lived in this area were Louisiana Creoles. Both Grandmama and Grandpapa were born in Louisiana. Like their parents and grandparents, they were rooted in New Orleans traditions and cultural upbringings.

"Mother," Grand mama's mother, lived in the Theme neighborhood. Mother was raised by her father's French family. She was Indian and French. Grand papa's family background was African and European. The whole family would ride the streetcar along St. Charles Avenue near the Garden District to the height of Mardi Gras. All of my older aunts would dress

Closing Chapter

in their Indian headdresses and skirts. Even Grandmama wore a feathered band. In the aftermath of the Hurricane Katrina, most of St. Charles Avenue escaped the flooding. I sat at the window for two hours after I had gotten the call. I was embracing the light in the bedroom. I began to go over everything Cicely said. The nursing home called around eight thirty at night to say that they were transporting Mama to the hospital. Mama was having problems breathing, Cicely said between her sobs. Cicely and Tony, my youngest brother, still lived at home with Mama too. Cicely was told before Mama died to allow Tony to stay at home because he had nowhere to go. They met the ambulance at the hospital. Cicely called Mama's doctor, who met them at the hospital. The doctor said he would keep Mama overnight. Cicely received a call later: "What happened when the doctor came?" Now she was boo-hooing and not explaining what had happened to Mama. "Bella, come as soon as you can. We need to lay Mama to rest. Come as soon as you can, please," she repeated.

"I'm leaving today, Cicely, as soon as I make arrangements." Cicely didn't say it, but I knew they didn't wait for the doctor to come to the hospital. "I'm coming to Mama's funeral." As I put the phone softly on the hook, the tears began to flow, and so did the memories. How many generations had come and gone? Was the value of family measured by what it loved? Mama loved her mother, and she loved my firstborn. I knew these two things were absolute. There are not many things of which we can speak with assurance, and this I knew.

My mama and Aunt Tamar were named after my grand mama. They were close, which is something I didn't share with my mama in my childhood. Did I succeed in getting close with Mama? Yes. I became a friend, a daughter, and one who grew to respect the woman who cared for me. Mama helped mold me into the person I had become. Mama could be uplifting, or she could be the truth that broke you. I just didn't know where or how to find that happy medium between us. At the end of our struggle, I could claim that I had been through an ordeal of finding love and coming out on the other side of happy. I had done my best to prove my love for Mama without playing some kind of trick on myself. Have I survived? Yes.

I was engulfed by awful feelings of sorrow and lost. The shadow of death had turned my night into suffering, and turned my mama out like the dead of old. When I had made the decision to move to New York, she was not pleased, but my grand mama had been a factor in my making that move. I never told Mama that I had discussed my plans with Grandmama, because I felt it would cause tension between them.

Mama did not want me to take my children. Why couldn't I live my life? But the inspirational message once again—"Baby, you are different"—gave me the courage to make the move to New York. Did Grandmama give this same heartfelt inspiration to her daughter? I think not. Mama never got her freedom.

I left anyway like a thief in the night, knowing I was leaving Zoe in my mama's care. I never got Mama's blessing. My youngest daughter, Danielle, was one. I left for New York. Jacob asked his mother, Mrs. Ina Rose, was happy to care for Danielle she soon became Mrs. Rose's love bone.

I had been dating Jacob Rose for a while when I discovered that he was born in New York City His father was still living there. Jacob couldn't find work and was worrying his mother to no end. I told his mother that maybe Jacob would be better off if he moved to New York. It was also a way for me to get out of New Orleans too. Mrs. Rose was kind enough to keep Danielle while we got settled in an apartment of our own. I joined Jacob a month later in New York. I took the bus, and it was the first time I had ever been outside the state of Louisiana. I was starting a new path for my life.

My path was directly before me now. I was realizing that a dream, a wish, or a prophecy was manifesting. My journey had begun. I was overwhelmed by this revelation instead of being fearful. Freedom and the thought of a new life had strengthened my resolve. Throughout my life there would be many more prophecies and dreams that would manifest themselves. Jacob was the love of my life and a means to an end. Jacob was the reason I would live my life in New York.

Zoe was two years old, and my life was out of control for a time. I was pregnant again, I didn't want another baby, and I was still living under Mama's roof. I tried everything I could to get rid of it. LeAnn, my girlfriend, had brought ginger root for me to drink and then had me sit in a hot tub; this should have made my period come. It didn't work. I had another baby, which I didn't want. *Lord, help me, please!* Mama told me "give him to his father." I did. I wanted to be with Larry, who was returning home from the military. We tried to make it work. Mama always knew it wouldn't.

Larry (his heart anyway) didn't come home to me. Something else had his attention, and I didn't have a right to ask. Something else had my attention. I just adjusted to life, as it was. I was pregnant with my daughter Danielle. Larry and I tried to make it work. We only made a baby.

My son was raised by his father.

Danielle was born out of my loss of love. I didn't know love. But love overflowed from Danielle to me. The relationship didn't work out. Larry married and failed to tell me, until one night when I had taken Zoe over to his grandmother Hazel's house. I was met with a slap across my face and a gun being pushed in my chest by some woman who told me that Larry was a married man and the child I was carrying was not his. As I was turning the corner to leave, Cicely was coming in my direction. I told her what had just happened, and she marched me back to Mrs. Hazel's house. She banged on the door for Larry and his new wife, Dorothy, to come outside. If she wanted to pull a gun out on someone, pull it out on her. No one ever came out. Those were the times. With all that I experienced, I knew that I loved Cicely, my baby sister. Cicely always took up my fights. We were like twins.

After Danielle was born, Mama introduced me to Jacob, a friend of my Aunt Linda, one of Mama's sisters. Aunt Linda was dating a guy named James. James was an up-and-coming black businessman who did well. Mama thought Jacob would be a good catch. I stopped dating after I found myself alone, twenty-one, and with two children. It seemed that with every confession of love I became pregnant. Jacob was a breath of fresh air.

I found myself searching for freedom once again. I had lost my self-respect. I was out of control with no safety net to catch me. I was looking for a love that would carry me into the future.

After giving birth to Danielle, I didn't go back to work right away. I moved back home. With plenty of time on my hands, I became part of the soap opera club. I stayed home and talked about other family members with Mama after she came home from work. Conversations Mama brought back from Grand mama's house were always informative. Grand mama's house was a haven for the family.

My mama's best friend was her mother, and the two of them could really call people out. Mama missed her mother more than anyone knew. When Grandmama died, part of my mama died too. Mama's mind sat in a dark place.

I think Mama's Illness was part of her suffering the effects of her own mama's death, not wanting to get any better, faulting herself for not taking better care of her mother or retiring early to care for Grandmama. They were as close as Mama and daughter could get. They were best friends. They could be like schoolgirls discussing everything.

Mama told me the story of the time she and my grand mama had just given birth to daughters only a day apart. Maya, my older sister, was born on my grand mama's birthday: July 5, 1945. Linda was born on July 6, 1945. Grandmama had to be hospitalized after Aunt Linda was born. Mama, who had given birth a day before, would nurse both her daughter and her sister on her breast until Grandmama was well enough to come home. Aunt Linda would not attend her sister's funeral. Did she remember this was the sister who nurtured her and fed her on her breast for two weeks?

*Closing Chapter*

There had been bad energy between Mama and Aunt Linda. They had not spoken in years. Mamma said Aunt Tamar had been the orchestrator. The issue concerned the purchase of Mama's house and whether Aunt Linda had any financial gain because her name was on the deed. Linda had not seen or spoken to her sister in over six years.

Chapter Two

# Coming Home

I was starting to talk to myself out loud. Hours had passed. I woke James and told him the news. "James, you awake? My mother just died."

"Baby, I'm sorry." He turned over to embrace me.

"She died sometime this morning. I didn't think to ask any questions. I just got off the phone with Cicely. I told her we are on our way." James sat up on the bed. I was still thinking about the fight between Mama and Aunt Linda.

I would see my mama's lifeless body for the last time. I wanted to recapture her life when she was alive—memories of yesterday. Mama had done many things. I could now see her life stretched out before me. For the sake of family, Mama would do almost anything that was in her power. Yes, God took all she was and placed in her hands the fruits of her labor, which were her six children. In the end that was all she had; that was her contribution to the world.

The memory rushed to the forefront of my mind, and I let it play out when the phone rang. "Hello?" This time it was Lip, my brother.

"Bella," he said.

"Yeah," I responded slowly.

"Cicely called me." Through his sobs and tears, he said it again. "Cicely called me and said Mama died this morning sometime in the early hours. She said she didn't suffer any. She just closed her eyes when she looked at her."

That was not the story she had told me. I didn't question it. He was crying as loud as Cicely had, as if they had just gotten beatings. He was heartbroken.

I shouted, "Lip!" I needed his attention, so I called him by his nickname. He had not used it in the seven years since he came to New York.

No one called him "Lip" but family. "We're going to be leaving sometime tonight. Are you coming with us?"

"Yeah, I guess I am. We'll get there late this evening, right?"

"Yeah, so pack enough for the wake and the funeral. We'll get there about six o'clock in the evening."

Lip was the second son and had been in some trouble during his young life. He had gotten himself into so much trouble that Mama and Daddy had felt that he needed to enlist in the military to keep from spending time in prison, because jail was where he was headed. Lip enlisted in the air force after high school. He was stationed in Hawaii and trained as a firefighter. He didn't write home often, so Mama was bothered if she didn't hear from him. She worried about her sons all the time. Lip would be forgiven for many things, even stealing Mama's jewelry. But Lip had disrespected Mama and the family. Mama never left family out. What you did to one, you did to the whole family.

Anthony was the youngest. He broke Mama's heart when he started to do drugs, cheated on his wife, and had children outside his marriage. She would say he was her greatest disappointment. Tony was a person who would get in where he could fit in.

Father's heart's delight and my mama's joy was Eddie. He had become the man Mama could be proud of for a while. Mama worried a lot about what would become of Eddie, but he, like me, had his own plan of escape. He enlisted in the air force after a year in college. Daddy and I were in the kitchen the morning he left. Eddie had not told anyone but me. Daddy asked me, "What are you up this early for?" Daddy gave Eddie a questioning look. "What's going on that you're up at five thirty in the morning?"

"Pops, I enlisted in the air force. I leave this morning at seven o'clock."

"What? This morning?" Daddy asked, with choking sounds slowly taking his breath. Daddy's speech was slow and deliberate when he said, "You know you're going to kill your mama with this news."

Eddie said, "Pops, you tell her." Eddie left without kissing Mama good-bye. Eddie and I hugged and kissed. The Allen Cab driver's horn woke Mama. I saw Mama standing in the front door.

Eddie left in the dark of the early morning. I blew him a final kiss and turned to face the music. Mama was heartbroken for a long time. All the time Eddie was in the military he sent allotted payments to Mama.

Once Edward came home from the service he married, moved away, and became a holy man of God. He no longer came by to visit. He felt that her house was no longer decent for his family. This hurt Mama, but she got over things pretty fast.

Mama could recall how much she had done for that sister or this brother; my mama would say, "They owe me more than they can hurt me. After all I've done for them," with her voice rising to a shout. My brother Edward stayed away for years. There was always this sorrow. You could feel it. Like time it got better, and Mama and Eddie found their way back to each other.

Mama's boys were now home from the military. My brother Phillip became a firefighter and Edward a mailman. For a while things were peaceful, and Mama was always excited about what was going on with her sons.

My brother Lip had fallen back into his troubled ways. This broke my mother's heart. He served his time and returned to the community. He found another good job and married for the second time, but the trouble won out again, and he lost everything he had. He moved back in again with Mama.

Mama called me one night crying, asking me to take Lip in because he had gotten himself into some trouble and some men were looking for him because he owed them money. I did as Mama had asked. I took my brother in, gave him a place to live, and took care of him until he could take care of himself, never asking anything.

That's what family does. That's what Mama did. Now he was crying his heart out. What had he given? How much Mama had cried for him, like the night she had asked me to take him in. He now felt abandoned, a saga in his life that played back and forth. Sitting on the bed, I wondered if I should go back to sleep. James was up. He went to tell Zoe. I looked out at where the tree in front of the bedroom window once stood. The branches were not the tree. Rachel was no more, not as I had known her. There would be no more phone calls or time spent fighting over differences of opinions.

My heart hurt, as if it was forcing itself though my chest. I could not take in a deep breath, only exhale. I thought I was going crazy, I had once before. But now was not the time. "Please, let me just take a breath! Mama!" I shouted at the top of my lungs. I could not hear my voice. "Mama!" The tears begin to flow, and I released my breath. I let go.

I remembered Mama was timeless and everywhere. Mama no longer connected to the physical but to my emotional and spiritual frequencies. I wished so much in that moment that I had the many letters and cards that I had written over the two years that she had spent in the nursing home. *Mama, why did you give Cicely my letters?* In truth the cards and letters were not as important as the act that was done and how intense it made me feel. I knew this feeling would last far beyond and endure. There would be no relief in which my soul could find comfort.

I had been in the backyard playing on the swing set Daddy had brought. Beverly, Mama's younger sister, was perched on the swings. Cicely came outside and demanded the swing I was on. I let her swing for a while. After I told her to get up and let me swing. She stopped the swing and got off. As I was starting to push off, she hit me in the back with all her might and knocked me forward off the swing.

Cicely ran up the back stairs into the kitchen. A few moments later Mama called me into the house and showed me Cicely's arm, where there was an awful bite. I got a whopping that day with an ironing cord. There was plenty of history between my sister and me. Our history was much like Aunt Tamar and my Mama, from the stories Aunt Tamar told. "Your mama was lazy and mean. Never did her chores or babysit the younger sisters and brothers." She had shared this story the morning of Mama's seventieth birthday party. It came out of nowhere. I thought it was hard to believe, but then again, was it?

Aunt Tamar said, "I know about your relationship with your mama and the letters. When you were here in October, visiting, your mama said, 'you fought?'" She said, "Are you worried about what you've written?"

I broke in, "I had told Mama that I felt the letters were personal and private. She told me she had given Cicely the letters to take home because there were too many of them. The shoe boxes were piling up. Why did she not give them back to me?"

"Your mama told me, "Cicely doesn't give a damn about reading those cards and letters. Your mama said, 'Cicely can't read so why is she bothered?' Bella, your mama was sugar and salt, a mean person, honey."

My aunt could see I wanted to end the conversation, but Aunt Tamar just continued to tell met things that should be kept in the dark forever. "Your mama said you think your sister destroyed your letters. Only you would think something like that."

I had asked Cicely what she did with them. "I put them in the basement," Cicely said with a very nasty attitude. "Zoe can get them when she comes to get her stuff." Her answer was discomforting, at best.

I sighed. "Why can't I come by?" I didn't get an answer. Why she didn't give them back to me I still long to know. I had many questions. Maybe she would. I hadn't gotten the letters yet, and we hadn't fixed what had been broken. Could we start again fresh? My soul had grown weary.

I will never have those cards and letters to recapture the moments I wrote them. Mama and I had always written letters and cards. She had saved many twenty-year-old letters. I had written them when I had left home. When we were on the cruise, Mama gave them to me. The letters were before Mama's time in the nursing home.

In one of the letters I had written, I had asked Mama, "Why would you leave all you have to one child when you have six children?"

Mama looked at me and said, "I have not given Cicely anything. Cicely and Anthony will still live in the house."

I felt anger toward my mother and my sister, knowing it was a lie. Cicely had put Tony out at the request of Cicely's sons.

Mama could have given me the letters. The chaotic influence now softened in proportion to the degree of love that I had for my mother, which was authentic. Mama was gone now. I no longer needed to be depressed. I was angry, and it felt a lot better than the depression. Those feelings no longer mattered, because what was there to be depressed about? My mama was gone. I was becoming emotional from the experiences in the reservoir of memories. I couldn't figure out if my memories were healing or morbid scars lost in pain. I just agreed with the mind right now. I knew that I was choosing, to be an observer of my thoughts.

Cicely never learned the true value of family possessions. How can you when you have been abused for many years? Cicely didn't realize there was a name for what was happening to her. Cicely must have seen it as normal. After she married, her husband continued the abuse. There was not a weekend that went by that she did not get beaten by her husband. My brothers tried to intervene, but Cicely would have none of it. Her husband continued to beat her.

Zoe, my oldest daughter, had not cried either, like me. I guess she was in another time and space at the moment. I called my daughter Danielle, who had heard the news already. She was feeling heartfelt pain. Tears began to flow freely. "Danielle, we're coming home. We're leaving tonight, baby. I know how much you loved your grandmother." I hung up the phone and placed it on the bed.

Danielle and Cholet had been living in New Orleans for some time. I missed my daughters dearly. I told them to expect us Thursday evening. Zoe came and sat on the bed. "What did Danielle say, Mommy?"

"She told me she got a call from Chris, your cousin. She called about 3:00 a.m."

I didn't know if Cicely had called Delaine, my baby brother Tony' ex-wife. My mother had grown very close to Delaine during their trouble marriage. "Well, when did Aunt Cicely call you, Mommy?" Zoe asked. "She should have called her sisters and brothers first, huh?"

"At this point, Zoe, does it really matter?" I asked. Cicely was more like Mama then any one of her children. Mama's passion was always to seek that which made her feel important and needed. In the same way, so did Cicely.

Danielle and I talked about my seeing Mama for the last time. On that last visit Mama had looked shiny. Mama had told Danielle that she was going home. Zoe, Danielle, and Cholet had been there all day with Mama. It was one of our better visits, and I was looking forward to our next visit.

Mama was looking better the morning I had seen her., but she hadn't mentioned that morning that she was going anywhere. I had been fighting with Maya about taking Mama out of the nursing home. Mama had been asking about going home lately, and she had the nurses call my older sister and tell her she wanted to go home.

When I asked about it, Maya replied, "Mama didn't know what she was talking about. There would be no one to care for her if she did come home."

How would she know Maya had not been to the nursing home? Zoe and Danielle would be the only ones to visit in the evenings.

# Chapter Three
# Mama's Quiet Days

I would spend the morning with Mama whenever we visited Zoe, my oldest daughter. Cicely had long since taken possession of the house when Mama when into the nursing home. Mama was always happy to see Zoe. She was her first grandchild. And the joy of her heart, my daughter, had come to lavish her with love and care that she didn't receive from her other grandchildren. They had seen the example their mother had set—not to get too close or share affections freely. It was sad at times.

It was as if Zoe was the chosen one and she lived up to that honor and gave all she could to make my mother comfortable. As for my older sister's children, whatever love they professed to have for my mama was unseen when she entered that nursing home. Their love had become a legacy of lies. Now Cicely's children saw my mama as their mama, for all that she had done for them.

When life should have brought her comfort, she was caring for Cicely's grandchildren. Mama's house was being used as a personal day care. Zoe also had lived with Mama off and on. Cicely's sons never spent the time or considered that even the simplest action they took, like visiting their sick grandmother, was a way of giving back.

There was this big family meeting where we all came together to discuss Mama's failing health. The meeting was to be with Mama and her children, but again Maya wouldn't come, so her children came to offer their opinion. Mama's health wasn't going to get better. She wanted everyone to take her seriously now that she had become housebound, but she needed others to take her out and help her get around. Mama was very proud. Asking for help was not easy.

Zoe knew her cousins better than anyone. Who would be there for Granny, and who would not? "Mommy not one of them," she said. "They are too much like their mothers."

Mama was there from the day my first baby was born. Zoe and my mama became very close, and Mama became a great influence in her life, so much so that at times I could clearly hear my mother's voice when Zoe would speak on certain things that may have happened.

If there was ever an opportunity to let my daughter express herself, this was it. "Zoe, are you okay?" I asked her.

"Granny's dead, Mommy, and I don't know how to feel. I don't know if I can say I'm losing my mother or my grandmother," Zoe said.

I said, "Choose what she was to you." She was losing a very loving grandmother. "Say what you will," I told her. I knew Zoe thought of my mother as her mother; she spent many summers visiting Mama.

Zoe spent four years of high school living with Rachel, my mama. I do not think role playing was what we lived to do but become the role we were to play on life's stage. I told myself my mother and daughter's relationship was abounding in love. It was the kind of love my mother had for her mother. You have to understand the kind of love that flows from reverence rather than respect.

Zoe could never really know Mama, as I had known her. My daughter grew up in the shadow of her wisdom; she could never be able to know what I knew about living in the reality. Zoe was born that cold December and lived upstairs over Grandmama and Grandpapa. She was born into a world I was attempting to exclude. "Let Mommy tell you a story about my mama. When I was a little girl—I guess I was maybe nine—I remember one night when we didn't know if we were going to eat any dinner. Mama was in the kitchen with Grandmama, and all of us kids were running around, playing underfoot. Mama told us to go outside in the backyard and play. I went and sat by the back door near where Grandmama would always sit, sewing a quilt made from old clothes. Mama asks Grandmama why Grandpapa wouldn't give her money to buy food. Grandmama said he didn't want to feed her children too. My mama went into the middle room where Grandpapa would sit in the dark with a Bible. Grandpapa never learned to read well, but he knew the Bible stories. I don't know what my mama said when she had gone in that room, but that night we all ate dinner—Grandmama's kids and us. I later found out that my mama had to borrow the money to feed us all, including Grandpapa's kids.

Years earlier Zoe had heard the story from her aunt Maya. Maya had a different feeling about the experience. Maya said Mama should have taken us and gone upstairs instead of feeding everyone. Mama would have to pay the money back. "Your granny, Zoe, was everybody in this family. We have always had to share my mama." I decided to tell another story, as there were many concerning her granny. "Great Aunt Linda was living upstairs, where we used to live, in the house on Esplanade Avenue. Aunt Tamar then told my aunt Linda to have her sister Rachel, my mama, pay to remove her from the deed so that she could have money to move. This was the reason Mama and Aunt Linda had parted ways. Aunt Tamar sold the house and had both sister and brother evicted. Your granny let uncle Robert come live with her. Linda moved out, as well, after Mama paid her to have her name removed from the deed. Zoe, Granny has done a lot with so little for so many."

At times Mama would do for all of them. After years of my mama living upstairs over her mother and father and helping to pay the mortgage, putting food on the table for all of us, where was Aunt Tamar then? Aunt Tamar had left the family far behind after she married and had nothing but resentment for her childhood and many a complaint about how we were being raised. But she was always reaching for the stars, and that was a good thing.

Aunt Tamar never talked with my mother about what to do with the family home. Mama said putting everyone out and selling the house was not what should be done. Mama had looked after everyone. What were they going to do now that Aunt Tamar had power of attorney? Mama, being sick, would give money to help her sisters who were struggling to keep their gas or electric on and rent paid. Aunt Tamar evicted her sister, Aunt Linda. Mama had opened her door not only to sisters and brothers who were in need but their children, as well. Then there was Mama's baby brother, who was incarcerated. Mama made arrangements every weekend for Grandmama to visit her son, and Mama didn't own a car. But every weekend for four years they visited Uncle Robert.

When Mama had brought the house at 4720 St. Charles Avenue, her sister Aunt Linda moved in. It was a streetcar ride to Mama's job at Loyola University. The memories surrounding Mama after she signed papers and the movers had taken only Mama's belonging they had left my belonging. It was evidence that I was not making the move to the new house. I was to share the upstairs apartment with my sister Cicely and her husband. Aunt Rose moved in with my mama, because she didn't want Grandpapa to know she was being abused by her live-in boyfriend. Grandmama was disgusted at how he treated her daughter. I could go on and on about the aunts and uncles. Mama did so much for so little in return.

Indeed Aunt Tamar did as little as possible and expected noting in return. Mama said Aunt Tamar would comment that all she had to give was advice, not her money. It was not her decision. "What good are words when you are hungry?" Mama shook her head. Only after my aunt had sold everything and put Grandpapa in a nursing home did she say she was making Mama the matriarch of the family.

They ended up in probate court. I laughed to myself when Mama told me. "What a joke!" The family reunion hadn't been held since Mama had gotten sick. We had to accept that. Even Great-Aunt Agatha, Grandmama's baby sister, didn't step in to carry on the family tradition.

Aunt Tamar and Aunt Ellie were the two who orchestrated the sale of the house and put Grandpapa in the nursing home. "I see what it all means now, Mommy," Zoe said. "Granny was the glue that held this family together. And now what are they going to do? Have they all forgotten? They have to remember who's been there even after Grandmama passed. They were dependent on Granny, your mama," she said.

Zoe remembered things as I had. She always watched, always sitting on the corner of whatever chair in which my mama was sitting. Zoe was sucking her thumb and rubbing my mama's arm. She reminded me of me, how I would sit at Grandmama's knees and suck my thumb and rub her leg. Zoe, after hearing stories about my mama's siblings, said, "They are all selfish, and they've been that way for a long time—the whole family. All of them are selfish. I don't remember any of them. And we don't get to choose the family we are born into. I'm leaving right after the funeral, after I get the last of my things from Granny's house." She started down the hall to her room.

I packed a bag and sat it outside the bedroom door. James called down the hall to Zoe, "You need me to carry down any luggage for yourself."

Zoe brought her bags to the top of the stairs, before she went to take her shower. I turned the television on to catch the morning news. Nothing got my attention. Doubt was beginning to challenge my beliefs, my faith, and my hopes. I wanted to stay positive, but I knew that in a moment my thoughts could determine how I would feel. I wanted to cry or scream. I got up and turned off the television. I just looked into outer space.

I was on a mission. I understood how Zoe must have been feeling, the pain about Mama and those who Zoe felt had not given of themselves as much as Mama had given of herself to them. She watched what was going on with Mama's children, and I watched her interactions with her siblings.

Mama discussed how she felt about what was going on in her home. An incident happened at Mama's house with Zoe and my sisters and my brother that resulted in my daughter having to be rushed to the hospital after she received a terrible gash across her wrist. Shortly after that, Zoe moved to New York and moved in with her sister Danielle.

Zoe had tried moving back to Louisiana several times, but the relationship had changed greatly between Mama and my daughter. I believe Zoe found out that her love for her children was greater than theirs. Somehow on that day Zoe became a threat. Zoe had begun relaying my mama's feelings openly. My sister Maya and her husband had lost their home, and "they" Maya and her husband moved in with Cicely, who, at the time, lived next door to Mama. "It was always the drama," Zoe said.

"Mama had many problems laid at her feet, with them living so close," I said. The burdens must have been heavy to bear. Mama had to be a strong woman whose breath was being sucked from her very soul. She gave and always made a way for others by taking from others what was needed.

I think the pressure—the worry of the family's well-being—added to my mother's illness. I think Mama was the bond that held the family together. I was wishing for a new way of being. Grandmama was like a river that collected all that entered its path. Zoe had moved back home to pay off some loans. She had been on her own for a while. She had moved back to New York two years earlier. Mama had been living in the nursing home for nearly two years. Zoe, Matthew, and I started out for the airport. Our flight for New Orleans was around ten thirty in the morning.

We pulled out of the driveway that cold early December morning. We settled in, with Lip behind the driver's seat. The

*Closing Chapter*

car started the slow journey to the airport. Remembering my mama Rachel had spent her time on this earth. It hadn't been easy raising six children on her own. Mama helped rise her sisters, and brothers. Mama had help from my daddy, but Mama prided herself on never being on the welfare system. Grandpapa never got cash but had applied for the government food subsidies.

    Life was not easy, and my mother always took less for what she truly gave. But we kids never knew we were poor. We had a television. When it came to raising sisters and brothers, as well as her own children. Only as I got older did I begin to express how I felt. Mama's sisters always seemed to need something from my mama, but no matter what state my mama was in, she never seemed not to have enough that she wouldn't give to them. This made her content. She always said, as Grandmama would, "What do you need with friends? You got all your aunts and cousins to play with." We were never allowed to let friends in the yard. Things aren't always as they seem when you're young. I had been living inside the illusion.

    Pulling onto the highway, the car sped up and so did my thoughts. We didn't talk much; we just said what was needed at the time. Being lost for words, we were focused on the purpose before us. I settled back in the front seat and let my mind carry me away. On Easter Sunday in 1959, we all woke up early. The night before, Mama had wondered if we would have new clothes. But it turned out to be a glorious morning. Daddy had come through. He told Mama to have us girls meet him.

    My oldest sister Maya, Cicely, and I met Daddy at Burstein Furniture and Department Store on St. Charles Avenue. We had to catch the bus. It was the first time my sisters and I had been anywhere together other than when we walked to school. We walked from Esplanade Avenue and caught the streetcar to St. Charles Avenue. The store was in front of the bus stop. Burstein's was crowed and full of furniture. Daddy met us as we came through the double doors. We walked down the narrow aisle, making our way through kitchen sets and end tables. The tall, skinny black saleslady wore lots of makeup and glasses that hung around her neck on a gold chain. She stopped at a table with nylons, socks, and packs of undergarments.

Against the wall were nice ladies' suits and other tables with slips and bras of all sizes. Maya told us to find our size. "What size?" I had never had a bra before. "Mama told me to get both of you a training bra." I smiled to myself as I meditated on that childhood moment. That was also the year Cicely and I stopped dressing alike. Mama had always dressed us alike, because we were so close in age, and the neighbors thought we were twins. For two days we were Irish twins.

Mama's story began years before. It was a cold December night as I headed to the airport for home. But I felt a warm summer breeze. The sky was filled with wishing stars, the huge bright ones. The moon was so bright that it looked like a mirror reflecting the stars in the sky, with their twinkling light. I was four years old, and my mama was the moving force in my life. Who really knows why we have certain memories of places and moments? I knew I would revisit this place in my heart, and the stories that followed came to be the stories that my mother would have me keep—stories not written down but passed on at moments that you didn't think to remember until a time such as this. I guess you could say that I was opening a time tunnel. Space and time don't change; they're filled by experiences, good or bad, that enrich our growth. I was growing. I was filling time and space. And inside that space was peace.

The stories my mama had told me were deeply rooted in my heart. I always had reservations when recalling my mama's strength and virtues. These stories would become written words of my life. A time had come for giving truth. I now felt that the sentence of death was not passed on the dead but on the living. Yesterday I found it again—a walk through my memories.

We climbed to the back of the truck, as many of us who could fit, anywhere among the furniture. I found a seat on top of the old wooden bread box. With my father's financial help, my grandpapa bought a house on Esplanade Avenue. My mama, with her three children, were still at home with her mama and grandpapa. Mama was twenty-three years old.

As the truck pulled away from the curb and the old house faded into the night, I remembered that it all began there. I was four years old. The truck moved through the streets, passing the neon sign, yellow flashing streetlights, and fast-moving cars. Coming off the expressway, the truck leaned as it turned those corners. It caused us to dance from side to side. Six of us took up spaces where we could see through the cracks in the board from the sides of the truck. We laughed and held on for dear life. It was like we were moving out of town. The ride was long and thrilling!

The truck slowed down and turned onto a quiet dark street, with its dimly lit streetlights in between trees. There were other children out in front of their houses, with the grown-ups sitting on the porches. After a while my eyes adjusted to the bright streetlights that were in front of the houses. Grandpapa finally pulled up and came to a stop. I looked through the cracks of the boards on the sides of the old truck, and I could see this brick house with a long walkway, porch, and two front doors. There hadn't been a porch at the old house; it was just a few steps up to the front door. The house we left had different streetlights and was dark at night. We had ridden away from that place. I thought about the kitchen and the cold floor where I would sit under the table and suck my thumb and rub my grandmama's leg, where the warm inner calf met the thigh. Even now when I get cold I will hold my hands inside this warm place, and sometimes the thought leads me back to moments that conjure up sweet emotions. And I'm there again sometimes with a smile or watery eyes.

Being four had left deep impressions in my mind and stories my soul had long kept. Now we had a front yard and a porch. I never knew Grandpapa couldn't read. When we were young Grandpapa would sat out on the porch and with the Bible read to us. Most of his stories were from memory. Papa learned them from church. I held many bittersweet memories with a smile. I loved my grandpapa. But I resent what he did.

Chapter Four

# My Mama's Papa

Almost everyone in the family was very afraid of Grandpapa. He was mean, yes, but he also was loved. Grandpapa was a short dark man who stood no more than five feet seven, and Grandmama was five feet nine. Grandpapa walked softly and carried a big stick with two leather strips nailed to each side of the big stick. He hung it at the back door, and he used it often on us kids.

Grandpapa would come looking for us if we had left from the front of the house after the streetlights came on. As we got older, into our teen years, he would bust up many a basement blue light dance that we would have lied about going to. I don't know if Grandpapa enjoyed whopping us with his homemade whip. Grandpapa did it because he liked being in control over all us kids. I realized that Grandpapa was doing only what he knew to do. I learned not to get whopped.

He was not educated, so he had limited ability to discipline without using physical force. If a man was to go to jail for abuse, Grandpapa was a good candidate. Grandpapa also came into good fortune; he was able to purchase a grocery store. Money he took from one of his daughter's husbands. The family had plenty of food after that. I think life answered one of Grandmama's prayers after years of locking the food away. Now Grandpapa owned the neighborhood grocery store, the Thurston's Market.

All of the younger ones had Saturdays to work if we wanted to. Most of us took and gave away candy to our friends.

Grandpapa soon tired of us. My Aunt Carmen, Aunt Brenda, and sister Maya worked in the store with Grandpapa. Grandmama hardly ever went to the store; she more or less didn't care, because she didn't see any of the money. Grandmama still cooked basically from scratch. Growing up, I loved her homemade ice cream and root beer soda. She didn't like processed foods. Sugar, flour, cornmeal, salt, and baking powder—that was her shopping list. *Oh, I can taste the buttered biscuits.*

My mama was born Rachel Thurston. Her mama was born Tamar Perris, and her father was born Paul "Papa" Thurston. Tamar Perris, my grandmother, married Paul Thurston Sr. on June 20, 1926. My mother was the fourth child of fifteen children. She had ten sisters and four brothers, and she was the second girl. Her oldest sister was her mother's namesake, Tamar. Paul Jr. was the second son, whom she called "Brother."

Mama's oldest brother, Carl, the firstborn son named after Grandmama's grandfather, had died in infancy. He was eighteen months old. He had been crawling around on the kitchen floor when he swallowed a tiny piece of glass. When my grandmama went to change his diaper, it was full of blood. They rushed him to the hospital, but she waited in the waiting room so long, and he died from internal bleeding.

He had lost a lot of blood. Grandmama's dress was soaking wet with blood while they waited to see the doctor. Mama said that sad story always came up whenever anyone would ask how many children Grandmama had. My mother always spoke of that story with her mother's sadness. Where her papa had been the afternoon her brother was rushed to the hospital, no one knew. She told the story as if her mama was telling it, and she was telling it to me. Grandpapa drove a taxi for a living to support the family, and Grandmama was a day maid. My mother could tell those stories as if they had happened yesterday.

*Closing Chapter*

Mama would tell a story with all the antics that made it exciting. Mama would imitate their movements and the way they talked. She could make you laugh and cry. Through Mama's stories I knew my daddy helped Grandpapa with the down payment to buy that house. My mother told that story every time Grandpapa would say things like "This is my house" or "You need to keep your kids quiet up there."

"You wouldn't have a house if it wasn't for Ed Smith," Mama told him many times. Mama knew where Grandpapa's good fortune had come from. We lived upstairs over my grandmother and grandfather all through my childhood and most of my young adult life. The time would come when I would need nothing outside myself.

I found spiritual hope early with spirits that played inside my head, dreams that I would manifest. Most of the time I would meditate. When I was a little girl, I would daydream about my life and fantasize about the moments. There were times during the hot summer months when we were able to go to the Fair Grounds, a community swimming facility.

I would go underwater and hold my breath for as long as I could, look up, and see all these colors. As I rose to the top, the colors would be circling the people. We were allowed to go to the Fair Grounds; this was my most sacred place. We all learned to swim. We all had to go together—my younger siblings, my aunts, myself, and my sister Cicely. Those days were good; everything about that time carried enthusiastic expectations. I had learned how not to get beaten with the leather strap by Grandpapa. My sister Cicely had received the worst of Grandpapa's punishments.

Grandpapa stomped on Cicely's hand as she tried to hide under the bed. Grandpapa beat her. He knew Mama was going to be very upset, because Cicely's hand had swollen so much that she had to go to the hospital. Thank God it wasn't broken, because Mama said Daddy wanted to hurt Grandpapa. Grandpapa never beat any of us from that day forward.

# Chapter Five
# Mama's Love

Edward Smith, my father, had a man-to-man talk with Grandpapa. We grew up not only with family around us but the love was plentiful. I had the only party that Mama had given any of her children, when I graduated from Webster School. I invited all my classmates.

My aunt Beverly and I decorated the backyard. We put up the blue lights and string paper. I put up a banner with my name on it. What I didn't expect was for Daddy to buy me a congratulations cake, two tiers with chocolate icing and strawberries all over it. We had chocolate ice cream too. *Oh, man, I remember it like it was yesterday.* It was the first time in the many years that we lived on Esplanade Avenue that any of the neighborhood kids had ever been inside the house. That was always a big no-no. But that night the house was crowded with friends and family.

The music and the night's festive mood swept me away. I was the only one who ever had a party. My daddy paid for that. Friday nights were reserved for the family bid whist card games. All my aunts and uncles would play well into the night. My sister Maya and my younger aunts made their way to Dance Land, a popular place for the teens. I sat on the front porch and waited. It wouldn't be long before fighting broke out between two of my aunts or uncles. Sometimes there would be blood, but the police were never called.

My first two children would be born on 4024 Esplanade Avenue. There would be four grandchildren born upstairs. My mother never left the nest. She bought a house with the help of my father after the three rooms became too crowded for her six children and four grandchildren. My sisters had moved out after they had babies, but not me. Even though I had a job and was attending junior college, I wanted to move with Mama. Instead I stayed on Esplanade Avenue. It didn't work out, because Cicely moved back in and I had to share the three rooms. We didn't get along because of her husband.

Daddy decided that I should move in with Mama in the new house. It was always quiet, because Mama was never really there. Between working and always stopping at my grandmama's house, you could always find my Mama at 4024 Esplanade Avenue. She was always checking on her mama, not wanting her to want for anything. She knew her father all too well. Grandmama was her only concern. If anything was missing, Mama would have known. There was never much time spent in the new house. Mama, being like her mother, had her sister move in, as well. It was as if Mama needed to be around her family.

She always needed to see that her mama was okay. Then she would come home, get on the phone, cook, run her bath, and go to bed. The next day she would get up and do it all over again. Mama was a moving force. She didn't own a car, but she never stopped going. The bus was her way of getting from one point to another. Daddy moved into the new house, but that didn't last long, because Mama couldn't take Daddy being gone every weekend and coming home late on Sunday nights. Mama was never home either except the week after she was off from her job. Daddy would come home from work, go into the bedroom, get a change of clothes, take a shower, and go out, if not cook dinner. Daddy was a quiet man, always deep in thought.

Mama was always on Esplanade Avenue. Daddy didn't have to ask, "Where's your mother?" because he knew. Mama stopped asking about Daddy, because she knew. What an arrangement!

Neither of them wanted any compromises. It was not the first time that things didn't work between Daddy and Mama.

Daddy lived with us for the last time on Esplanade Avenue. After about a year, I came home from school and found Daddy taking his fishing poles and his gun collection from the house. Something just told me that he would not be back soon. When Daddy was home, there was an abundance of love and laughter. Daddy was a joker and a tease. I embraced it. I hate teasing now.

Daddy would come to the school whenever there was a problem with any of us. He took the time. When we were sick, he took us to the doctor. He told riddles and sang sailor songs. He would always play with us after our baths on Thursdays before he would leave to go to the gambling house for the weekend. I thought Daddy had two jobs.

Mama spent her free time with her sisters, going to the Cardinals baseball games. They would come home after a game with some of the Louisiana Cardinal players, a local team made up of police. Mama knew when Daddy would not be coming home. Uncle Nelson found out about it, and he waited for Aunt Tamar to come home. Then he called Grandpapa and told him to "come get his whoring daughter." As for my daddy, he either never found out or he didn't really care. The family was in an uproar. Uncle Larry, who was married to my aunt Ellie, waited until the Friday night cards games to bring it up.

Grandpapa got Aunt Tamar that night. Uncle Nelson wouldn't let her take the girls with her. Aunt Tamar stayed but one night. After that we rarely saw our cousins again. Grandpapa told Grandmama she was as much at fault as her daughters, because she had gone to some of the games.

Grandmama would cook whenever the players came to the house. They loved her fried fish and potatoes. Daddy even moved us away in the midst of what was brewing between Grandpapa and Grandmama when he discovered that we were being ill-treated at the hands of Grandpapa.

That didn't last long, because Grandmama had talked Mama into moving back to Esplanade Avenue. I felt sedated and emotionally doomed after we moved back. My sister Maya became more defiant with Mama and started to drink and smoke cigarettes and marijuana. She would watch from the corner at Play Right Lunch Counter, where we all hung out after school, and double back home when Mama would leave for work. None of us wanted to move back to Esplanade Avenue. We were happy to have Mama to ourselves. But that didn't keep them from visiting often. We didn't do many things with the rest of my aunts anymore after we moved.

Mama's sister Beverly was a year younger than me, born a week after my sister Cicely. We didn't walk to dance lessons at the YMCA anymore on Saturdays, which were twenty-five cents a lesson. My daddy started to drop me off, and I would see her there. Daddy enjoyed Mama more too. We even had a telephone. We were a family like Aunt Tamar, Uncle Brother, and Aunt Ellie. It was fascinating to become part of the summer caravan going to the family's cookouts.

When we had moved from Esplanade Avenue to Burgundy Street, it was nice living in the two-family brick house. It didn't have a long hallway like the three rooms on Esplanade Avenue. When you came to the top of the stairs, it opened to a living room with a small kitchen off to the side with huge windows. The bathroom was small, without a tub. It was like a circle. The two bedrooms were off a small hall at the other end. There was a small sink and a toilet in the bathroom. We would bathe in an oval tin tub that hung on the back porch. We lived on the second floor, and our neighbors on the first floor owned the house.

Maya, Cicely, and I shared a room, and Daddy and Mama had a bedroom that they shared with Lip, our new baby brother. That was another reason my mama moved from Esplanade Avenue. Mama and Daddy had another baby. Eddie was three and still wouldn't walk. But he was potty trained; he would crawl to the bathroom.

There were five of us plus Mama and Daddy. The wonderful open apartment was beautiful and quiet—not like the three rooms on Esplanade Avenue, where there was no living room.

But now there was and a television that Daddy also bought for us. My joy would be short-lived. We had changed schools too. Mama enrolled us in the Cole School.

Daddy had bought a newer station wagon and wanted to teach Mama to drive the old one. Mama would have none of it, so he gave the station wagon to Grandpapa. Daddy would sometimes give us a ride to school. We didn't live that far from the school, so we could walk, but Daddy wanted to be nice and let us ride in the new car. Mama hadn't found a job. She left the five and dime when we moved, so she went with Grandmama and Aunt Ellie a couple of days a week to do day work. Aunt Ellie would drive. We would come home at lunchtime. We got an hour, from twelve o'clock to one o'clock, and we got out of school at three thirty. Times had changed. I tried to shake the memory about education.

I knew when we moved back to 4024 Esplanade Avenue that I would be bused to an all-white school. It would be different for us. Daddy was a high school graduate, and he stressed the importance of education to us. Daddy knew that there was a lack of understanding, because he knew Grandpapa was uneducated.

My daddy came into my mama's life, and she had a baby. When they met, she was still living at home with her mother and father. My father was older than my grand papa by seven years. Daddy had met my grandfather at a dice game. My father was a part-time loan shark. He would lend money for quarters on a dollar. Great-Uncle Bill lived the life my daddy knew a lot about. One dreadful night when Uncle Bill almost lost his life, my daddy stepped in and took the knife from a man who caught Great-Uncle Bill cheating. As a little girl, I had heard stories about my great-uncle, about the things he had done to the women in his life—awful things he had done to two of my aunts when they were girls. My mama had told the story.

On Saturday morning she and her sister Alice went to Uncle Bill's boarding house to clean, as they did every Saturday, to get a few dollars for the movies or whatever they might need. Uncle Bill was Grandpapa's older brother. He was the oldest of four.

Grandpapa had one brother and one sister. Great-Uncle Albert was a stepbrother. He grew up with Grandpapa and his sister and brother. Great-Grandma Queen, Grandpapa's mother, had the nickname Ms. Q. She kept company with a few gentlemen, and Great Uncle Albert's father was a regular visitor. Great-Uncle Bill, Grandpapa's younger brother, didn't have very much respect for his lady friends, but he did for Mother Queen.

Great-Uncle Bill used the women who came into his life. He owned the house he lived in, plus the Good Time House, where he would steal my mother's youth. He was a businessman, and he didn't force the ladies to do anything that they did not want to do. Great-Uncle Bill's ladies never stood on the corners. They were escorts. Mama often mentioned that Grandpapa would drive city politicians to Great-Uncle Bill's Good Time House. That was why Great-Uncle Bill could afford two homes.

Great-Uncle Bill raped my mama, and nothing was ever done by the law or my mama's parents. Great-Uncle Bill was strictly into making money. He had no idea that later in life the evils that he committed would find him when he was old, weak, and penniless. Uncle Bill was now in the grips of his great nieces. The daughters of the girl he raped. Cicely and all of us kids became his worst nightmare. I could see dark shadows do this flamboyant dance around him as Cicely would whip Uncle Bill with Papa's belt.

I could see shadows following people all the time but never that many. Sometimes I would see them just walking around, day or night. Mama had said I was seeing spirits. I didn't take it seriously or believe that was it. As time went on, things became clear to me. I could never cast a spell, but I could always for some reason read with some intention. I loved spending time with a good book or a good story. Grandmama would always say, "No one tells a story better than my mother."

Mother was always proper with her way of speaking. She always corrected all the children in the house. Mama told her about a dream. I had dreams that frightened me terribly. "Great-Mother, you know about dreams too?"

"You see the spirits."

"What?" I asked. I was no more than five or six years old.

She asked, "You see colors coming off people?"

"Doesn't everyone?" I asked.

"I've seen spirits walking about too." She smiled, bent down so she was face-to-face with me, and said, "Honey, child, don't let them trick you ever. We live in a strange world, baby. There are things that go on beyond your senses." I knew what Mother was referring to.

Mama had been haunted all of her adult life. Something happened to Mama, and she didn't have the support or love to help her work out the demons that tormented her after her youth was spent raped and broken. On this Saturday morning, my mama was cleaning one of the downstairs rooms. Uncle Bill had quietly come up behind her, put his hands over her face, and said, "Guess who."

Mama said she wasn't afraid at first, but when he didn't take his hands away from over her eyes and instead began to put his weight on her to force her down on the bed, her fear exploded. Her uncle Bill forced her face into the mattress and held it there with one hand as he took down her pants and panties with the other hand. She knew then what was coming. She tried her best to free herself, but the more she struggled, the deeper he pushed her head into the mattress. She could hardly breathe or turn her head. After he had finished, he simply walked away.

Mama was fourteen years old. She ran up the stairs, out of the house, and into her sister Alice's arms, unable to get the words out about what had just happened to her. She could barely walk now. When they got home she told Grandmama what Uncle Bill had done. She called the cab company and told Grandpapa to come home right away. He came home at ten o'clock, the regular quitting time after his shift was done.

She heard her mama and grandpapa yelling at each other about what had happened to her in the front room of the three-room shotgun house. Mama said it got quiet after a while, and she didn't hear another word. Grandmama never came out of the front room that night.

The next morning before any of them could get up, Grandmama heard what had happened after hours. Mama said her grandmother had come to the house and asked her sister Alice to tell her what had happened that Saturday morning at Uncle Bill's boardinghouse. Great-Grandmother asked Grandmama why she had not had him locked up for raping her daughter or called the police when Grandpapa didn't come right home when she called.

My grandmama sadly said that if she had called the police on Uncle Bill, he would leave her. It wasn't that Grandmama loved Grandpapa so much. She never portrayed herself as someone who was fully controlled by a man's passion or lust, but having so many children was not always a sign of many nights of making love. Sex looked like it played an important role in their marriage. However, I seen love that was based on vows a experience that Grandmama felt and I believed was her tribulation because of my Mama's rape.

Grandmama had nine kids at the time, and she told her mother she was afraid that she wouldn't be able to care for them if Grandpapa left her. She feared the state welfare department might step in and take her children from her. Mama said her Mother was so mad at her daughter that she slapped her across her face. She began to tell her how Grandpapa had kept her barefoot and pregnant from the minute she married him, because he didn't want anyone else to want her.

Great-Grandmother went on ask her how she could stay with a man who had been locking food away from her and the kids and who only put out what he thought was enough for the day while he was gone until night. Grandmama had nine kids and little money to buy food some days.

Grandmama did the best she could with what she could find. Her "butter bread and beans" became famous. Mama had said after the kids started to come, Grandmama rarely went out. She did day work and she would come home and cook and clean too tried to go out partying. Grandpapa was out at his brother's or his mother-in-law's after-hours house every Friday night. Identifying with what seem to be cruelty forward his children Grandpapa separated his action as for why he would not be home with the family. Grandmama learned to do wonders with very little. My Grandmama believed that with good deeds something manifested for the good of all involved. I wanted to feel something good. There was a simplicity operating in my thoughts, bringing good to my experiences. I didn't want to think. I wanted to sleep. But the past continued on.

Grandpapa drove a taxi for a living, so money was always an issue. Great-Mother would always step in when times got really hard. I think she never liked the fact that Grandpapa kept her pregnant every two years. It was as if all he wanted was a warm body to fill his sexual needs. I think the day my mama was raped by Great-Uncle Bill, their relationship was destroyed forever. Grandmama discovered that Grandpapa cared more for his brother than his own children.

Grandpapa, trying to make things better, would then start to do more, but it wasn't enough. He would take Grandmama out on her birthday and New Year's Day, and on Easter he would take all the kids to his mama's church. Grandmother said he was mentally abusing her, and now she was letting him let his brother rape his daughter. Who knew who else he did this to? I didn't want him in this house anymore. How could I look at him after what that bastard did to Rachel? She was only a child! Of all those whores he had there, why did he have to touch her daughter? *What are you going to do? I'm calling the police now! I want him locked up!* Years later Great-Uncle Bill suffered for the ugly thing he did to my mama.

"You will do nothing!" my grand papa said. My mama said her grandmother was a woman to be dealt with. You didn't want to mess with her. Great-Grandmother swore she was going to kill Great-Uncle Bill. Grandmother "Mother" was well respected in the community. She led a nocturnal life, mostly kept to herself, and always carried a gun in her purse and on her person at all times. She was of a different cultural background. Nothing was done to Uncle Bill. And even more suffering and pain would come later. My great-uncle Bill would die penniless behind the furnace in the basement at 4024 Esplanade Avenue.

The night my daddy came to Grand papa's rescue. Grandpapa brought my daddy home with him t and that's how my mama met my daddy.

Mama said my daddy and my grand papa would form a close relationship. It wasn't long after that Mama and Daddy began their relationship, and not with Paul Thurston's blessings. Long after he got to know my mama, and very soon after Grandpapa became good friends with my daddy, he got a job at the Heritage Coal Company, where my daddy and his brother worked for some years.

Chapter Six

# Mama's Babies

Mama's world had become magical. Her life with her expression were sudden emotions that was reliance of my own childhood

When I was four years old we moved to the new house. I watched my mama's life unfold at the house on 4024 Esplanade Avenue. "Okay, let's get this stuff off the truck!" I could hear as Grandpapa jumped from the passenger's side. My Uncle Robert stepped from the driver's side. My uncle Wilbert pulled up in the station wagon behind the truck. Grandpapa was heading to the rear of the truck. We all climbed down and ran to the porch of the new house. I looked back and saw my older sister Maya was close behind, calling my name.

Mama and Grandmama were getting out of the station wagon. Mama was holding my baby brother Edward and pulling a big suitcase from the backseat. Bedding and other stuff was packed back there too. My uncle Nelson, who was married to my aunt Tamar, my mama's oldest sister, had pulled up behind my uncle Wilbert's car. It was like a caravan.

My Grandmama got to the door, and we all pushed, wanting to see. "Open the door, Grandmama," my mama said as she pushed her way though, carrying my brother Edward on her hip. Grandmama unlocked the front door, and a new world opened. Mama said, "Okay, move back, you babies. Come on, kids. Get back." When my mama first spoke, she treated everyone like babies. Then her voice would get loud, and she treated them like kids.

I went back down the steps and watched as everyone carried things into the house. Aunt Carmen, Aunt Rose, and Aunt Jean had ridden in the car with Uncle Nelson and Aunt Tamar. We called Aunt Tamar "Auntie Ta." I knew at that time that Auntie Ta didn't live with us, and neither did my aunt Ellie, who was with Mama when Great-Uncle Bill raped her at the tender age of fourteen. Aunt Ellie hadn't been home for some time. She would leave home for periods of time.

She had run away. I didn't know what that meant, but she would be at Great-Grandmother's house every time she ran away. Grandmama had said none of her girls were safe, because Grandpapa refused to do anything about his brother. Uncle Bill kept coming to the house, knowing everyone knew, saying my Mama was a little tease.

I didn't really remember Aunt Ellie at the old house. She had come home, and Mama said "she married early" just to get away. We moved, and she was there when we pulled up to Esplanade Avenue. I had developed this attachment to Aunt Ellie, but she wasn't there very long. Carlene (Aunt Ellie's cousin and Grand papa's sister's only daughter) and Aunt Ellie moved out. Mama talked about that a lot. None of that mattered to me. That night was the first time that I had been up so late. I watched the grown-ups talking and working together, filing in and out of the front two doors. Mama started asking who was sleeping where and with whom.

Each of the apartments was to be shared by the family. My mama started gathering blankets, sheets, and pillows for the beds. We kids never slept with pillows. It was as if you knew that you had to be a certain age to be awarded a pillow. Later I knew Grand Mother had brought them. The still night air was hot, and when the wind stirred, I could feel the heat. Everyone sweat as they hauled the heavy furniture. I felt delighted and full. I followed everyone as they walked down the long hall into each room, placing things here or there. I recognized the furniture from the old house. Where was the coal stove? Shouldn't it be in the bedroom too? It was missing.

I explored all the rooms and the basement, which was the largest room I had ever seen. The concrete floor covered the entire basement. The big black furnace was many times bigger than the coal stove on Esplanade Avenue. It had to be to heat this big house. We kids would grow up roller-skating in the basement and playing red rover, jump rope, and tag. Later Grandpapa had rooms built in the basement, and my aunts moved from upstairs, leaving my mama, my sisters and brother, and me. After the move, everyone settled in.

We had bologna sandwiches and a cup of Kool-Aid that night. I slept with my mama in a twin-size bed that night. My daddy got my mother an account at the furniture store where he did business. Daddy bought a new bed and dresser set for the new house. Mama bought a sofa and breakfast set.

My aunts and uncle moved downstairs. This was an upgrade from sleeping in a twin bed with my mama and my sisters. In the other bedroom was a full-size bed where Aunts Sweetie, Carmen, and Jean slept. In the middle of the room was the coal stove that had a warm glow late in the night and the smell of the coals as they burned slowly.

Uncles Marvin and Robert slept in a full-size roll-away bed in the kitchen. Mama couldn't believe how much I had remembered about my life. I was only three going on four and very much invisible. My world was inside my mama's world.

I would keep most of what I knew until I was far away from New Orleans. That's when I told Mama what her baby brother, Uncle Robert, had done to me. She held the phone and asked, "Why didn't you tell me this when he was molesting you, Bella?"

"Mama, I don't know."

We didn't discuss it any further. I wasn't afraid of my uncle. I didn't understand why I was letting him do what he was doing.

I was six when it started and eight when it stopped. One day Uncle Robert just went away. When he was arrested, the molestation stopped. It was something that was happening to this body, not me. I was alone with this person. I didn't really know him, but I saw him every day. He was a part of my life, a part of my family. Uncle Robert would give me candy every day, so I trusted him. The first time it happened, I didn't understand.

I'd seen Grandpapa give Uncle Robert, along with Aunt Barbara and others, many whippings. He could make you scream and shout if you didn't follow his rules.

The belt hung behind the back door. It was two long black belts nailed together on two sides. The worst I've seen Grandpapa give was the day he beat Uncle Robert in the front yard. All the memories about Uncle Robert weren't pleasant. I'd even felt sorrow for my uncle. I have to say that I never hated him; I just despised the act. My memories of those years had all but faded into the background of my thoughts. I didn't think about it.

Today people talk openly about child abuse and molestation. I recall the time I was home, visiting, and was at my sister Maya's house. Uncle Robert had been living with her, after he was released from prison. He and my brother-in-law Carl worked nights at a soda company. I was visiting early in the morning. Sis and I were going to go shopping and have lunch later at Blimpies.

I heard his voice, and my first thought was *Does he remember?*
"Niece, how long have you been in town?"
I said, "Hi, Uncle Robert."
"So, you left Louisiana, huh? You like Harlem?"
"It's good, Uncle Robert."
Maya interrupted, "I'm going to get dressed, Bella."
"Hey, Maya, I wanted you to fix me an omelet," he said as he took the chair she was just sating in.
"No, you don't," she told him as she exited the kitchen.
"How about you, Bella? Can you cook?"
I gave him a weak smile. I wanted to tell him, "Do you know what you did was not okay?" He needed to be sorry for what he'd done. But instead I cooked him the omelet. Maya and I went shopping. When we returned I didn't go back to Maya's house and never mentioned Uncle Robert again.

Chapter Seven

# Mama's Family

My mama had always lived with her mama and grand papa. She had six children living upstairs until she purchased a home of her own. Mama, along with her old sister (my aunt Tamar, who was a senior and two years older than my mother), had gotten pregnant in high school. Mama said Grandpapa was so upset about them both being pregnant that he asked them how they could be carrying on with boys when their own mama was still having children.

My grandmama was also pregnant with my aunt Linda, so Grandpapa had both his wife (my mama) and my aunt to take care of with babies coming. Mama went to live with Grandma Queen who was one half white European one half black. My aunt Tamar went to live for a short time with the Grand Mother Mother" who was half French and half Indian. They both knew their grandmothers very well, as they all had to see after Grandma Queen and run her errands, because she was too heavy to do any walking. Grandmother had a housekeeper. Aunt Tamar got the better of the deal.

My grand papa would drive his mother around in his cab. Grandpapa later worked for Heritage Brothers Coal Company. Grandpapa would give my mama and her sisters' instructions for whatever needed to be done for his mother. Mama said, "I hated going to her house, because she abused us." Grandpapa would do for his mama by getting his children to do it. Mama said Alice Thurston, "Grandma Queen," was a beautiful short woman with hazel eyes, so she named her daughter Hazel. Mama said, "She was named for her eyes." Hazel had long, soft, wavy hair and light caramel skin.

Mama said her father's mother was stern when they were children. Grand papa's mother was like this all the time. I was very afraid of her. Nothing we did was ever good enough. My mama knew this firsthand. Great-Grandma Queen believed in "hitting for not moving fast enough or pinching," my mama said. My mama and Aunt Tamar had to cut Grandma Queen toenails each month.

She delighted in surprising them with a pinch for no reason at all. My mama got plenty of them when it was her job sometimes to wash her feet. Grandma Queen was too short and fat to reach her feet. Her daughter Hazel refused. Paul "Papa" Thurston made sure his children took out his mama Queen's trash and kept her walkway clean.

My great-aunt Hazel named her daughter Carlene. She was an only child. Carlene was the same age as my mama. Carlene also refused to wash and take care of her own grand mama's feet. It was said there was enough evil in their house with the three women. Women were strongly rooted in this family regardless of the men they married. They could hold a grudge. Payback was only a matter of time.

Great Aunt Hazel made "Hot toddies the cure for all." It contained bourbon, lemon juice, and honey. "Sweat it out," Grandma Queen would advise. If you got pregnant, she had another remedy for that, and ladies in the neighborhood would seek her out.

Mama's cousin Carlene, like her grandmother Alice and mother, had beautiful hazel eyes. "Oh, they come from the Thurston side of the relatives," Great Mother would say. Carlene and my mama were very close growing up. They were first cousins. All the females in Grand papa's family had very light complexions, but Grandpapa and his brother Albert were the darkest, the color of coal. My great-aunt Hazel was Grand papa's only sister. Grand papa's brothers never had children. Uncle Bill and Uncle Albert had plenty of girlfriends with children, and we welcomed them in. It was just the four of them.

Both my mama's grandmothers had after hour parlors on Sundays and sold beer and liquor. This was not unusual during the Depression. Papa's father brought beer from his mother that's how they met. He worked on the railway, laying tracks. Papa's father was Chinese and black. They barley got to know him, and he sometimes would bring his father, Papa's grandfather a Chinese man Mama said he never spoke with any of them. He was only home long enough to spend time with Grandma Queen when she was having a baby. Mama knew more about Grand Mama Queen Side of the Thurston family.

Grandma Queen's grandfather was a white man from Chester, New England. The relationship between slave and master produced children. The Thurston family in a will to Grandma Queen's mother Mrs. Eva all the descendants and those who followed would be freed. Mrs. Eva had known Mr. Williams Thurston who was an insurance agent for the rail road. He was a tall white man, with a head full of dark red hair. Mama said he never married her Great grandmother Grandpapa used the last name Thurston when he and his brothers and sister went to school. But Mama's ancestry stretched further back than Louisiana.

The story Mama told was that they believe Great-Grandfather was Chinese. Papa knew his grandfather as only Mr. Wills. His Grandmother would call him gentle Mr. Wills. Mama said Grandpapa and his brothers had to miss school most of the time to help their mother. Grandpapa had dropped out of school when he was in the fifth grade and his brother, Uncle Bill, was in the eighth grade. They were eleven and thirteen, respectively. They would steal coal from the coal yards, sell some, and take some home. This was during the Depression, and it was not an easy time for anybody, Mama said. Grand papa's mother would also find it easier to sell eggs under the cover of selling liquor to her white customers who came Saturday mornings.

As a young woman, Great-Grandma Queen lived with her mother, and her boys helped out by collecting coal from the freight trains as it was dumped into large coal bins. Uncle Bill would steal it, and Grandpapa would sell it to poor white people near the tracks where his grandfather worked. Papa's grandmother lived with the white family most of the year.

Grand papa's brothers Great-Uncle Bill and Uncle Albert grew up fast in New Orleans. Mama said, "Grandma Queen lived through many experiences." That lady could weave a story as my mama soaked her feet and manicured her toes. But Grandpapa never knew much about his grandfather's family. Most of those relatives were back in Old China. Papa's father's mother died when he was a little boy. One could certainly tell that Grandpapa looked just like his grandfather. They all had Chinese eyes and small stature. Mama also remarked, "Grand papa's mother was very light, and Grandpapa was born very dark, like her."

Sometime later, when she came to live in Louisiana, she had his younger brother Albert. My mama remembered only the names Mr. William or Mr. George, concerning Grand papa's great-grandfather who was white. But she couldn't tell if it was her Chinese great-grandfather or her white great-grandfather who left Grandpapa the land. Great-Grandmama Alice got names mixed up all the time, but never the details about anyone. My mama never met either of them. But there were lots of stories. This was the world of stories my aunt Jeanette and my mama Rachel grew up in.

My mama remembered the story told by her Grandmama Hattie, her mama's mother. Knew for sure there were no birth records kept back then. Mama said, "Grandpapa surely kept a record of all his children's dates of birth." The four eldest children were born at home. Mama's grandmother was half Sioux and half white. And mama's great-grandmother was full-blooded Sioux Titans. Great-Grandmother's father, Mr. Milton

*Closing Chapter*

Lofton, was Dutch. Hattie Lofton, my great-grandmother, was born around 1875. She was a beautifully frighten woman.

My Grandmama called her "Mother," so we children all followed and called her Mother. GreatgrandmotherHattie would tell us kids that Sioux Indians were really known by another name and that the whites took their words and way of life and changed the world of her mother's people.

They were a tribe known as Teton Indians along Baton Rouge, Louisiana, who were moved from Arizona and settled in Louisiana. Great-Grandmother's family lived on the Missouri Plains. Great-Grandmother Hattie's father, Mr. Milton Lofton, the Dutchman, worked with the Quakers on the Indian reservation, where lots of free ex-slaves were mixed Indian. Mama knew her great-grandmother Hattie didn't like black people much.

Great-Grandmother Hattie ("Mother") was tall, at five feet eleven inches. She had beautiful jet-black hair and a brown-golden complexion. She walked very slowly and looked around to see who was watching. She didn't live long. Mama told her story, as it had been orally told to her and, years later, orally told to me by Mother Hattie. I was thankful to have had the opportunity to have known her in the flesh. As the story goes, they settled in Quincy, Louisiana.

Great-Grandmother Hattie's two sisters, Bessie and Bell, were twins. The three of them could pass for white. Quincy, Louisiana, consisted mostly of milking dairy farms and cattle ranches back then. The slaughterhouses were where blacks, Indians, and poor whites alike worked.

The last name for the Dutch family was Welch, and they changed it to Lofton. "I can't recall his first name most of the time," Mama would say. But before she was done telling the story, his name would roll off her lips like honey spreading over hot toast. Mama would say in the middle of a pause, "Mr. Milton Welch—that was my great-grandfather." He was the Dutchman who was from Quincy, Louisiana. This she knew for sure.

The Dutchman had sent for Great-Grandmother. She and her sisters went to a missionary school near the reservation, where they learned to speak better English. They also learned skills such as sewing and dressmaking. She and her sisters took classes in good manners. Mama would laugh when she told this part of the story. They were very beautiful girls. They could all sit on their hair. The three oldest of seven children, Great-Grandmother would have four miscarriages.

Mama said that her grandmother always kept a decent job, because their father sent them to the reservation school. Grandmother Hattie and her sisters lived at this women's residence in Baton Rouge, Louisianan. My mama's Grandmama Hattie left the residence shortly after she arrived in Louisiana. She met and married Mr. William Patton. My mama's grandfather was a loving black man. Like her white great-grandfather, my mama loved them both.

Once they got to Baton Rouge, Great-Grandmother Hattie acquired a job as a day maid. Later Mama's grandmother acquired a job at the sewing factory, and one of the other sisters, Mama's great-aunt Bell, got a job as a department store elevator operator. Life was good.

Mama then told the story about her great-aunt Bell, who had taken the job under the pretense of being white. At the downtown department store, the manager who hired her thought she was a white woman. My mama's mother was sent to the store after work to meet her aunt Bell and borrow money. My Grandmama had a very light caramel complexion. She showed up at the employee rear door, looking for her aunt Bell, and was told no colored people worked there. They asked what this person's name was. Grandmama said, "Betsy Welch."

Mama said, "She was fired on the spot when they went and found her." Mama also said, "You can't hide from who you are." Great-Great-Aunt Bell left Louisiana for many years after that and went to California. She returned to Louisiana after some time.

*Closing Chapter*

My mama also would come to know hunger. My mama sisters and brothers growing up would go Hungary because; Papa would lock the food pantry.

Mama told that story with a cocky smile, and I shook my head. Well, it was now a fact that both these sisters had found themselves staying with their grandmothers, because they were no longer welcome at home. Grandmama was also carrying their next sister or brother, and this would be number eleven. The power to overcome adversity was on both sides.

The life my mama was born into was strange, not just a cultural tradition. She took accountability for the fact that the three-room flat she shared with ten other sisters and brothers and a mother and father was to become her children's home.

Mama didn't make the necessary steps to turn her hopes and dreams into realities. What was my mama's dream— having three children out of wedlock? My mama grew up in a household that was full of fabulous and strange people and very volatile times. All who frequented there used the side door that came right into the kitchen. Grandmama kept a beautiful garden along a path that led to a small grapevine. The gangway was used by all. Thirteen people lived in three rooms. She told of the sorrowful night that she was to leave and go live with her grandmother Hattie, which was far better than having to slave for Grandma Queen. There would be company for Mama at both grandmothers' houses. They lived quite different lives. My mama never talked about her mother's childhood.

Mama could remember the childhood stories her grandmother told, but never her mama. Grandmother said Grand mama's life would have been very different if she had not married Paul Thurston. Things would be different when my mama returned home with her daughter Maya. The time spent with her grandmother Hattie and cousin Carlene gave Mama a different view of her life, when it came time for the families to meet and talk about my mama and my aunt Tamar. Mr. Boney, Uncle Nelson's father, had said their son would do the honorable thing. Aunt Tamar and Uncle Nelson were married.

The Hopes' family wished something different for their son. Mama said Ms. Eva Hope would not approve of their son marrying. Mama said that they thought that Mr. Charles Hope's education came first. So there Mama was with a baby and no boy to marry. I think that was another devastation that my mama had to endure at the hands of a man who professed to protect her innocence and another who took her honor.

My mama would become broken but not a weak woman. She clothed herself in the magic of making stories. I loved magic too. When she would make-believe something, I would laugh because Mama knew somehow I knew.

It had started raining as we boarded the flight for Louisiana. I looked at my watch, and it read 3:42. The rain was really pouring now, and the wind was strong.

Lip took us through the stormy night with a funny story about keeping your seat belts on so you can live through death. Lip had been driving for a company, and he had to drop off physical therapy medical supplies. He got onto the highway, and the rain was not that bad, but a truck hit him and he rolled over three times across the highway. They had to get the Jaws of Life to take me out.

"I was lucky to be alive."

*What a story for a rocky ride on a plane,* I thought to myself and shook my head.

"Know what?" he asked as he leaned forward in his seat. "The seat belt kept me locked in tight, but it did more damage keeping me in that seat. Then that truck made me pee on myself."

"What a ride!" I thought it was at the lowest point that we could clearly see what life was really worth. "If we can see death coming ..."

Had I seen Mama's death in that nursing home? Yes, I had. My mama had seen death waiting, lying there in that bed day in and day out. I remembered going outside, walking around the nursing home parking grounds and crying, "Lord, show me your face in all of this."

*Closing Chapter*

Lip and Zoe were sleeping now, and the silence was beginning to blanket me with sorrow and consume my soul again. I needed to use the ladies' room. I got up and made my way to the bathroom. I shut the door and cried for what seemed like hours. I washed my face and made my way back to my seat.

"Do you remember when we were visiting Granny?" Zoe asked. "She was talking about going home," she said as I sat down to buckle my seat belt.

Thinking about Lip's story, I smiled. "Yeah, I do," I said, turning to Zoe.

"Well, this is what she was talking about."

I paused before I spoke, wondering if Lip and Matthew were listening. I drew in my breath and said, "It didn't have to be this way, Zoe."

"Mommy, she was ready," Zoe said as she rubbed my back. "I am going to miss her so much, Mommy," Zoe said as her voice trembled.

"I know, baby. I know. I know."

Zoe had lived with my mother all throughout high school and even before that when I had first moved to New York.

The sun was setting behind the clouds. The late morning was slowly giving the stage to the evening in shades of gray across the sky. Did the rain stop, or were we flying over it?

We made light conversation on the rest of the flight. Zoe was wiping the tears with the back of her hand. "She taught me so much, Mommy."

My grandson Matthew put his hand on her shoulders and told her Granny loved her too.

The car moved into the traffic as we were leaving the airport. The trucks played a picture in my mind of Lip rolling over three times. Ghosts of the past would not let me rest. Edward was driving slowly because of the rain.

We didn't eat much breakfast before the flight. I wasn't hungry. It was getting close to dinner.

"Are you okay, Zoe?" I asked.

"I really don't know, Mommy."

I really didn't know what to tell her either. I had resolved most of my feelings, but I didn't know if my oldest daughter had seen my mother as her mother. Zoe had lived with my mama throughout her high school years, most of college, and even after she dropped out of college for a while. She got a job at Loyola University, where my mother had worked for over thirty years. Mama had been working there before Zoe was born.

I was seventeen when I gave birth, like my mother. She had her first child at seventeen and was not married. I had no husband myself, but it was not because Larry didn't want to marry me (I found out later). Why would I remember that? There must be something I had yet to face in my relationship about my mother making my choices for me. I, like my mother, stilled lived at home. But I did manage to get my education and a job right away. I always measured myself against my mother's life. Now all I had was memories, many of which were faded.

On one of my visits home, I found Mama sitting at the kitchen table, crying. "Mama, what's the matter? Do you feel okay?"

"Honey, I'm fine. I was just thinking about my mama."

All day I laughed about something she said or did. I had my moments.

My mind shot back to the present. I had been measured out in bitter acts of memories. Today I decided to seek the center of myself, affirming my true reality, claiming my responsibility, and embracing it. Mama had a childlike faith, and she often told stories that, in her mind, happened because the family lived under a curse. When it came to bearing children, she was very fertile. Every time someone fell in love, they got pregnant, and most of Mama's sisters fell head over heels. The downstairs was filling up with grandbabies, as was Mama's house upstairs too. But Mama welcomed it all after a good cry. Her two daughters were only months apart in their pregnancies.

I went to school after the news was shared with other family members. Aunt Tamar had made it a point to say that Mama must see to it that I finish my education. She never continued her education, and she hoped that wouldn't be me after I had my baby. I always felt sorry my cousins had to listen to my aunt talk about how they should live their life and what was expected of them as contributing members of society.

Aunt Tamar wanted to be Grand Mother so much. I knew the loving, not the social, great-grandmother. Aunt Tamar always would tell the ant story and how the ant's life was nothing but the joy of work. That was a good rule of thumb, but she never really practiced the rule of the ants. Maybe she meant the bees. Now I could see her as the queen.

Memories were bubbling over, each crowding out the space in my mind. Some were coming to the brim, overflowing the substance of my being and I felt a chill. I shook my head and softly said, "Then she does make sense." When what you create comes into view, it becomes your story, your stage.

Cicely and I still shared a bed by the time we had our babies. Daddy had to buy another set of bunk beds for the boys. Cicely and I had bassinet for our babies. Ms. Angelina, our neighbor, had told Mama that I would make a wonderful mother because I was such a sweet girl.

I was a terrible mother. Ms. Angelina was wrong. I knew nothing about motherhood. When Zoe first came home I was weak. She was a beautiful baby. Zoe had a head full of hair, long eyelashes, and bright and happy eyes. I had gotten stitches and was very sore. I was depressed much of the time. Maya was ready to step in to help me. Maya would get up at night with Zoe, feed her, and sing her back to sleep.

When Cicely came home she would sing late into the night to her baby. My sister Maya had a beautiful voice. She sang in the glee club in high school. Maya performed at church and other events. Mama got off work too late for most events, but everyone else in the family who could be there was, and there were many of us.

I went back to school. When Zoe got a little older, and went to work. Maya babysat. She didn't have any children then. She had just dropped out of nursing school. Her best girlfriend, Rosella, who had a baby, was getting married. Aunt Linda and my sister Maya spent most of their time together.

One day out of the blue, Maya refused to give me my daughter, claiming I had given Zoe to her. I had to go downstairs and tell Grandpapa to please come upstairs and talk to her and make Maya give me my daughter. I think then our relationship changed. Maya stopped babysitting. I don't know really what kind of relationship we had before that night.

Mama started talking about the house becoming crowded and who was contributing to the bills. Cicely had married and moved into a rooming house. She was at Mama's every day with her son. Maya was home all day, and I had to get a babysitter. We were growing and moving in our own directions. Maya got pregnant. Mama started talking about buying a house. Daddy had moved out for the last time. I knew he wouldn't be back.

Chapter Eight

# Mama's Decisions

Danielle's house was dimly lit only from the porch light. It was around seven thirty in the evening. After greetings, Zoe and Danielle left. Zoe wanted to smoke; she couldn't do so riding with my brother Edward, who had picked us up at the airport. She lived in the moment. Zoe wanted to see her aunt Jean, her father's aunt, to tell her that her granny had died. We had arrived safely. It was becoming more real as I started preparing for the wake and funeral.

While Zoe was out, I unpacked my few things and shouted to Philip to take a quick shower and that I was taking mine too so that we could go to meet the family. Zoe wasn't going to Mama's that night. She was staying with Danielle. She said she would be there when we were done. She'd be back before we were to leave for my mama's house, which was now Cicely's domain. She had booked rooms for my brother and me at the Omni Hotel, where she worked, for the rest of our stay. I knew she was still worried about her own father, who had been sick for some time, and his aunt Jean wanted to see Zoe.

Mrs. Jean Black from the neighborhood knew my mama's family. For years she watched us grow. She and my mama socialized at the same neighborhood lounge, Mr. Jesse's Jazz Traven. How would she take the news? I wondered. They never really liked each other, I found out later when she asked to see me after the funeral. She told me why my mama did not want me to marry her nephew. I didn't know that Mama had forbidden Larry and me to marry. And the story goes on.

When I became pregnant, Larry Lee Smith asked to marry me. Larry's family had decided it was the honorable thing. I was pregnant with Zoe.

Larry had enlisted in the marines so that we could have a life together. We never got married, and he regretted enlisting in the military. She said, "I never knew the whole story, and I wouldn't know until now." What happened at the family meeting those many years ago, when my sister Cicely was only sixteen and I was seventeen? We were pregnant at the same time. It was a remake of an earlier time playing out on the stage of our lives. I played my mother's role of the unwed mother. My sister Cicely, who got married, played my Aunt Tamar's role.

Larry, my baby's daddy, came to my house with his mother, who lived in Milwaukee. Larry was raised by his aunt Jean and his grandmother, Mrs. Lillie Brooke. Larry was not a tall man, but he was very handsome.

Larry's mother was a short woman with very big beautiful eyes. Her skin was like gold. Larry's mother spoke for their family. "My family wants to know how the baby is going to be cared for. How are you going to get your education if you are having a baby? You can't live with your parents if you do," his aunt Jean said. Marriage was not to be written for me. My mama convinced my daddy not to allow me to marry the father of my daughter, but Mama and Daddy did sign for Cicely to marry Tommie Coles.

Looking back, I know that I shared a life that passed on traits. We were no different; we were just as we should be. Daddy felt that Cicely would be better off married, because she refused to go to school, and Daddy was about to send her to the same reform school for girls. My sister and I were in cycles of repetition. Cicely never got much education by the time she and Tommie met.

Cicely and I had gotten pregnant at the same time. Jean went on, but at this point I was no longer interested in what she had to say. It was as if now she was trying to say the decision Mama made concerning my life and what would be good for me wasn't. Looking back, I thank my mama for her foresight.

Mamma said that there would be no marriage for me and Larry. Cicely was moving out. And I was going to finish high school. Mama made me go to school until I started to show, and then I was asked to leave. I attended night school. My daddy paid.

I told Jean after she was done that my life had turned out fine, better than I could have imagined, and that what she thought was meant for evil had been a blessing. The reality was that Mama and Daddy had made the worst decision for my sister Cicely, who was abused throughout her whole marriage.

I softly said to her, "If we had gotten married, I would be taking care of a sick man who was addicted to crack cocaine."

Jean was breathing with contempt. Words didn't match the expression in her voice. "Oh! That would never have been if you and Larry were allowed to marry." Larry was suffering from a broken heart, and the drugs were the result of it.

I put the phone down and took a shower. Time was passing slowly. I was remembering the essence of my mama's life, which was intoxicating. I drank in every word Zoe was telling me. I had finished the call. I dried off, got dressed, and sat in the living room with everyone.

"Mommy, she wants you to come see her. She wants to tell you something about Granny," Zoe said.

"I spoke with her already, Zoe." There was an irony in that maybe there were many secrets that I really didn't know. What was it that Ms. Jean was trying to do? She knew my family, but she had not realized that this was a good time to have me go beyond my heritage and be stripped from the lies of the past about my mama. That no longer mattered. What she had said was an omen.

I had accomplished what I needed in the moment. It would have been difficult, if not impossible, to confront my mother. She was dead. To have someone bring doubts about her now was personal, too late. My mother was gone. The estrangement with my sisters was going to be enough to deal with. I wanted to concentrate on something that was positive. I wanted to reflect and to remember my mama in a light that I knew to be a beacon, always calling me forward.

I came into the kitchen. Danielle was fixing something to eat for her uncle Lip. I went into the bedroom and sat on the bed. I called Mama's house, and Cicely answered the phone, sounding more assured. The urgency was now lost. She was telling me they were at the house and the plans had already been done. If I wanted to come over tonight, it was okay. Shouldn't all of Mama's children be making the plans? I was thinking, *Tony, Edward, Maya, and Cicely.* I said Lip and I would be there within the hour. She said okay and hung up before I could say good-bye.

Chapter Nine

# Mama's House

Lip and I got to Mama's house at around nine thirty at night. I hadn't been there since the night my sister Cicely wouldn't answer the door. I rang the bell for the first time in over a year. Since Mama had been in the nursing home, the only communication I had with my sister Maya was over the phone. I never received an invitation to Maya's house when I came home for visits. On the other hand, I would call her, and she would come to Mama's to take me to pick up my rental car. When I came home we would have lunch, and once we went on a shopping spree, my treat. What happened?

Cicely and I gave each other only a civil "Hello" if she felt like speaking when we saw each other at the nursing home. Tony opened the door. "Hey, sis."

"Hi, Tony. You okay?"

"I don't know, Bella," he said as we hugged. Then we moved into the living room. Despite the dark, I could see the new hardwood floors right away. I came through the dining room, and the light from the kitchen shone on the hall floor into the dining room. I could see that the whole house was newly done over. Hardwood floors now replaced the worn slate hall floor.

Mama's house was remodeled, to my surprise, and Cicely never mentioned it. When I saw the kitchen I didn't recognize it. The kitchen was completely redone. Where was Mama's kitchen? The last time I had stayed at Mama's, Cicely had the locks changed, and she reluctantly let me in. She didn't like the fact that some of Mama's kids and grandkids had keys to the house now that Mama was in a nursing home and she had moved back h0me. She felt that no one should have keys. My baby brother Tony let me use his key, which she had given him, as he was still living there when Mama went back to the hospital for the last time. My mama's next stop was the nursing home.

Tony gave me his key the last time I stayed at the house after the lock was changed. I stayed in Mama's bedroom and slept in her bed. This eased the cost of a hotel during my visits home. That would be the last time I smell the scent of my mama. I didn't dare ask who had the house remodeled. I really didn't have to.

I think much of the changes that were being made were to bring Mama home at some point. I was hoping that was the case. If so, it must have been very hard for Cicely, for Mama didn't get to see the changes.

Now was not the time. I stood at the kitchen door, looking around. Cicely was talking to a couple of sisters from her church, and my older sister was sitting at the kitchen table with paper and pen in hand.

"Good evening, everyone." Cicely turned to me and said, "Mama went in peace. My mama was tired. She was ready to go home to her father's house. Amen." Cicely looked at me. "She's in peace now, sister."

A church friend chimed in, "Your mama knew the Lord, and she is resting in his breast, waiting to be carried home." She got up to embrace Cicely, who now was crying softly, nodding her head in agreement.

"Bella, Mama wanted to be buried in that green dress with the dark green trim. Green was my mama's favorite color."

"Hunter green was. I know," I said softly, the words vibrating from my tongue. I wanted to embrace Cicely and she me, like we did when she asked me to forgive her for some mean act she had just committed. I felt empty. I wanted to hold my sister, but

*Closing Chapter*

I didn't. I kissed her on the cheek. Maya never got up to greet me. As it had become a custom to embrace a family member upon greeting, I gave her a kiss on the cheek. Maya passed the obituary over her shoulder as I was still standing in the doorway. I read it silently and couldn't recall or understand the basics of what was being said about Mama's life.

I had spent long hours talking to Mama about her childhood as she lay in that nursing home bed. A new world opened as Mama told me stories that now made sense to me, when they hadn't before. I understood. The tears were not from what I was reading.

Mama had reminisced many times about her experiences. Mama was always taking account of her life. I asked questions when I felt she was in the mood to answer. Mama's mind was very sharp all the time. I continued to read what had been written. It wasn't anywhere near what an obituary should have been. So who was I to complain? The pallbearers were my sisters Maya's and Cicely's sons. I was not referenced or mentioned, nor were any of Mama's sons. Philip and Anthony were bewildered too but said nothing. "We felt the grandsons would be a better show for family," Cicely said with a snap in her voice.

I asked Maya if this was the final draft. She told me Cicely had already written it, and she was going over it. I felt a chill as my heart pounded in my chest. I knew well the emotion that was welling up in me.

Feeling the energy of the room. I sighed. "What are these days going to bring?" I asked, not knowing I had spoken. "What funeral home has Mama?" I need Information I have to pass onto my friends who want to send flowers. A church sister who was sitting at the table with my sisters Cicely and Maya offered to get the information for me. Neither Maya nor Cicely had it. They were busy trying to get the obituary written, and Cicely's nephew was doing the printing. As Cicely was on the phone, Edward came into the house, calling from the front door. "Hey, good evening." Everybody looked up. "Hey, sis."

"Hi" was the dry response from Maya. She had stopped writing for the first time since I had come in.

We were all there, the six children of Rachel Thurston. The six of us never shed a tear together. I cried softly but didn't shed real tears. We didn't do that in front of each other. We were there in body but not in heart. It might have helped if the church folk were not there. I wondered if we were all experiencing the same feeling. I felt we were unable to share our grief. We hardly knew each other anymore. I made my way around this foreign kitchen, asking for the phone book. Miss Church Lady had taken it from my brother, who was standing at the far counter next to the back door.

The kitchen was bright with a new floor, and the refrigerator had been moved. There was so much more room in the kitchen, Mama's favorite place in the house. *If only,* I thought. *A little too late now. Thank you, but no thank you. I can find it.* Cicely was going on and on about Mama and how peaceful she was when she last saw her in the emergency room, waiting for her doctor.

Cicely went into Mama's bedroom and brought out the green dress that I had bought Mama for the cruise we had taken almost seven years earlier. I was quiet, contemplating the decisions that had been made. My presence went unnoticed. I found that being invisible was a good thing. For the rest of the evening I focused outside of the sorrow that was filled only with guilt. I didn't know why, but I felt guilty because I wanted these church women to leave and let me have time with my family. *What is it with these people?* They probably never visited my mother when she was confined to that nursing home. There was a spiritual truth in the atmosphere. I could feel that faith had been abandoned. I wanted them to leave my family we needed our own prayer. We needed power of divine acceptance between us, not some church folks who were there only to report back to the other church sisters about what went on in sister Cicely's house.

How much did they really feel for the loss of our mother? The church folks were busy doing nothing but taking up space and making it hard for Rachel's children to share their sorrow and grieve with each other. I sensed that Cicely had them there for her protection from the truth that was now facing us all. But my emotions were the marker for what we were all feeling. If they left Cicely, we would have to face our past and what Mama had meant to us as individuals.

Small talk between Cicely and Maya left little to discern. They had already discussed in length what was going to happen with the wake and the funeral. Lip was getting bored, or he was tired of Cicely going on and on about being at the hospital with Mama. "We knew this before we got here."

"Where were you when she passed?" Lip asked. Cicely said that the hospital had called her at home.

Was I misunderstanding what Cicely had told me earlier on the phone? It didn't matter, any of it. "This was never the way I imagined we would be."

"Why?" Cicely asked in a tone of disgust.

"What have I done to be shut out?" I asked. I looked at the women sitting in my mother's kitchen. It wasn't Mama's kitchen anymore. We were acting strange with each other. There were no tears, just shouting and accusations. Tony just kept standing by the back door, lost in his own world, fixed on the television I had given to Cholet, who in turn gave to Mama, the only thing that had remained.

All of this had taken place in two years. Mama was on a fixed income or no income, now that she had been committed to the nursing home, and Cicely was waiting to go back to her job that she had left when she moved to Atlanta. Where did the money come from? Yes, I was curious. Why couldn't this have happened sooner, when Mama was begging to come home? Zoe later told me that Mama told her on that last visit that Cicely's son, the oldest of her four boys, had borrowed money from Mama to start his Creole Chicken and Shrimp Restaurant. My mama also told her that she would be coming home once the work was finished. Did Mama die before the earthly or heavenly work was done? The house was finished when I was there, around the same time Mama died. How long hadn't I known? What I did know was she never got to see it.

Mama had taken out a mortgage on the house. The house had been paid off for three years after Mama retired. She wanted to have a deed party, but she just didn't find the time. My mama took out the mortgage to help her grandson. Mama said Cicely had promised to make the payments. Whether Cicely or her son had been repaying the loan was questionable. Mama would call me constantly for money, but she would not always tell me what she needed it for. Now things were coming together. Time reveals all things done in the dark.

Mama never told me about the loan. Zoe did. Mama had told me about the roof leaking into her bedroom. I always did what I could for Mama. I never refused her anything. Now I realized how much I had scarified for Mama, how I had worked to prove my love. I struggled to fathom the amount of effort it took to say thank you to someone whom you blamed for abuse. I was learning in my sorrow. The person we see outside isn't the person inside. I wish I knew hard love then, but how could I? I knew nothing about the struggle. I hadn't growth up yet. What I have come to know is the result of a struggle. My mama struggled. Rachel Thurston lived her life and brought her children along.

Chapter Ten

# Mama's Funeral Arrangements

Once I got back to Danielle's, I knew I would not be able to sleep and that the dark memories I was keeping at bay would come busting forward. I didn't want to close my eyes. The shadows were busy. Every thought and every memory did a flamboyant dance and insisted on being recognized.

The words and image were haunting. *You remember! You remember! You remember!* I knew if I closed my eyes, the stories would play out on the stage. Danielle handed me a glass of wine and told me to relax. By now, it was late—later then I thought. We had stayed longer than we should have. I guess Lip and I were trying to oust the church sisters. They were there when we left. Lip decides to spend the night at his ex-wife Lorna's house. I told him to take the car but to be back early, as we were meeting them at the funeral home the next morning to finalize the funeral arrangements before the wake.

We all arrived in different cars. Lip and I were together, and my brothers Edward and Tony rode together. Cicely and Maya pulled up in Maya's car. The tension was cutting off the energy in the air, and none of us could find words to express ourselves.

Each of us looked tired. Our souls were consumed. I made eye contact with each of them, and each of them looked emptied of all human emotions, void of connecting to the sorrow that was in our souls. What looked like sorrow was nothing more than disgust. I don't think I had time to adjust my emotions before Cicely spoke up and said Maya had already picked out Mama's casket.

Edward asked, "When was that done, Cicely? Why didn't you call me?"

"What for?" Cicely asked, not even looking at him.

Edward didn't respond. He knew not to, from the look on her face. Cicely stirred with bad feelings.

We walked behind my sisters, who spoke only to each other. Ms. McLane, I could see, was feeling uncomfortable. Edward, Phillip, Tony, and I followed like tourists on a tour.

We all made our way down the hall, with Maya leading the way, carrying a shopping bag full of insurance policies. Ms. McLane, a short and well-dressed woman, showed us into a small office, and we all sat down to hear what arrangements Cicely and Maya had made. "How did everyone else like the casket your sisters picked?" the well-spoken secretary asked.

"Fine." We all picked the same word at the same time.

"The angels you picked to sit at the corners of the casket are removable," she explained. "So, there are six of you sisters and brothers. You need two more."

"Well, the oldest sisters and the oldest brother can have one. That's four. I know I'm going to get one," Cicely said.

"Oh, please, wait a minute," the secretary interrupted. "Maybe I can get two more."

In the meantime, she began explaining to us the cost of the casket and other services. The secretary informed us that the cost to have the hole dug would not be included in the insurance policy. That expense would have to be paid by us.

Lip interrupted and asked, "How much would that be?" before the secretary had a chance to finish.

Cicely hissed in a nasty tone, "You got some money?"

We all looked shocked. Forgetting where she was, Maya said, "Cicely, don't do that."

*Closing Chapter*

The secretary asked us to give her a moment and she would check. I searched my brothers' faces and then looked at Maya's face. She only looked down. Ms. McLane left the office to get the information about the cemetery site. It was not Renaissance Cemetery, where Grandpapa and Grandmama were buried. Zoe informed me of that. My mama would not be laid to rest where Grandpapa and Grandmama had been buried. "That is too far to travel," she said. Aunt Cicely told her. Ms. McLane returned to the office and wrote down the address for Lip. She went on to calculate the cost and ask what type of policy Mama had.

Maya, who was sitting next to me in the small office, turned to Cicely, who sat on the other side of her opened the grocery bag and pulled out a number of insurance policies Cicely also had a few policies in her purse, one being the leather-back policy Mama had earned after thirty years of employment at Loyola University.

I felt heartache, for I knew that Mama wanted to be next to her mother, whom she loved dearly in life. I couldn't bring myself to say anything. I didn't want to get into any disagreements with my sisters at the time.

I approached Maya in the parking lot after the arrangements were finalized. "Sis, we need to talk. I think we need to sit down and express some of our concerns, Maya."

"Okay," she said without letting me explain why.

I thought she would invite me to ride with her and Cicely to the cemetery so that we could talk, but she didn't. I got into the car with Edward, Tony, and Lip. "Bella, did you ask Maya about us getting together to talk? Because I don't have a clue about Mama's finances," Edward said. "Anybody know if Mama even had a will?"

"Yeah, Mama had a will," Tony said. "Mama asked my girl Elaine over to notarize a revised copy of the will at one time. I don't know if that happened. But Elaine also said something about a quick claim deed. I'll call Elaine," Tony said as we decided to get something to eat.

It was late afternoon, and the sun was turning a beautiful orange color. If only I could navigate my emotions better! I felt the warmth. I knew the two of them had been talking in secrecy before Mama died. Aunt Ellie was there the day Mama died. Cicely had called her before the church people showed up that evening, before I arrived. Cicely had given Aunt Ellie a lot of Mama's things that morning. Maya took a bunch of things home and came back.

I was so sick over Mama's death that I just went downstairs and lay down. I was surprised by my sisters. "I didn't think Cicely and Maya would have gone through Mama's belongings the same day that she died. I didn't believe it. When the news came about Mama, Maya acted like I was invisible."

"I know, Edward. I saw that last night when Lip and I got to Mama's house. We didn't talk much after the ride from the cemetery. Lip asked me why I didn't ride with Maya and Cicely."

"Sis, didn't you want to ride with your favorite baby sister, Cicely?"

"Their behavior is so out of place. Two of them took care of everything before you came in town, huh?" Lip had a way of making things worse than they were.

"I don't know, Lip," I said with some hope of things working out for us. There wasn't much time left for us to come together.

Chapter Eleven

# Mama's Lost Children

I had become somewhat distanced from my sisters after I moved from Louisiana. Whenever I visited home, there was never an invite from either of my sisters. I found out later on a cruise with Mama that the reason Cicely never came back to visit was that I didn't make her feel welcome. What a laugh! That was never a reason for us not getting together whenever I was home visiting. If I had to define my relationship with my sisters, it was in my mind, I guess. There once was, but I found it hard to define now. We were all grown women. My older sister had become, for a while, a second mama. A single mother had to work. She didn't raise her children on public assistance.

Maya, Cicely, and I had shared duties. Maya was responsible for us kids until Mama came home. When Maya wanted to go off and be with her friend, Cicely and I would play in the yard with our brothers Eddie, Lip, and Tony. Thinking of that, I sighed. "I wish we could laugh and tell stories about our childhood. There were many stories, enough to begin again." The one time we laughed and cried was when Lip was a baby. Edward turned over the bassinet, and Lip rolled onto the floor.

Maya was in charge, and we would sit on the front steps while Maya played jacks with her girlfriend Barbara. Maya knew Mama didn't like Barbara because her brother smoked marijuana and he liked Maya. I always promised not to tell

Mama when Barbara and her brother visited. As soon as Mama got home I would tell. Maya would be enraged. Once she almost knocked me over the side of the porch. I screamed for Mama, but she never came.

I started to remember how close the six of us were. Living upstairs over our grandmama and grandpapa was like having two sets of parents. Tony talked about the time Grandpapa had nailed up the doorway leading upstairs one cold winter, because Mama couldn't afford to buy kerosene for the heating stove in the living room. "Was it because cold was going downstairs and the heat was escaping upstairs?" Tony asked.

We all laughed but then stopped. That memory was laughing at the pain. We pulled into the parking lot of Renaissance Cemetery. Edward parked next to Cicely.

Cicely flashed a look at Edward and me. It was obvious to us that Maya had told her about the meeting. From the look Cicely gave, maybe this would not go well. We finished our business at the cemetery and entered the waiting area. The customer service representative informed us of the cash payment before the ground would be opened. Maya asked each of us if we had money. I asked what my portion of the fee would be. "I don't know yet. We have to divide the bill six ways."

"Okay, when we get back to Mama's house," I chimed in with a happy tone.

Maya looked as if she had smelled something nasty as she ran her finger across her nose. A gentleman approached us and asked if we were ready to see where Mama was to be laid to her final resting place. We all went outside to wait for the caretaker to take us to the area of the graveyard where they placed a marker for Mama.

Standing on the stairs of the office of the cemetery, Cicely kept looking away, not making any eye contact. She looked at Maya as if she was following her lead. Only two of us could ride. I climbed into the wide front seat of the truck next to Maya. Cicely and my brothers stood on the stairs. As we rode along the narrow paths, Maya, not turning her head, said, "Cicely doesn't feel like meeting at the house. She has people coming over."

I took Maya's hand. "Maya, our needs right now are more important than those church folks!" My voice was stern. Maybe I should have used tact instead of the aggression I was displaying. I could feel what she was feeling. We were a match. "After last night, sis, I need to speak. It isn't about fixing last night. It is about us feeling better about what is happening now."

Maya didn't respond. We rode the rest of the way in silence. We came upon a little hill where a young tree stood. I said, "That young tree will have plenty of room to grow and become shade over Mama."

Maya removed her hand from mine. I had forgotten I was holding it. We climbed out of the truck's cabin. Maya and I followed the groundskeeper down the little hill. I looked backed and saw Maya standing at the beginning of the little hill, afraid to make her way down.

I turned around, met her where she was, and helped her down the rest of the hill. Mama had worked hard on getting Maya an appointment to see a doctor about her knees. Maya could no longer push Mama in her wheelchair when she took her to see the doctor.

My big sister and I stood there. I felt weighted down, as if from a mother's sorrow. Maya had been like a mother. I looked from the corner of my eye as the groundskeeper explained the process to us. I saw Maya's aura for the first time. A warm pink enfolded us, and I was once again transported back to a moment when she was like a mother lion protecting her babies.

Maya came home early that day. She found the Cicely, Edward (who was the youngest at the time—he was three and still not walking), and me sitting in the hall downstairs at Grandmama's. "Why are you all sitting in the hall?"

Edward stood with hands outstretched as Maya picked him up. Maya had been drinking and smoking pot wherever she and Aunt Linda had been after glee club, or maybe they didn't go.

"Grandmama told us to sat out here until your mama or sis came home," Cicely said.

Maya looked puzzled and then angry. "Daddy was supposed to come. Why didn't you go upstairs? They're eating in the kitchen and didn't let us eat," Cicely said, standing up and walking to the kitchen door. "Why didn't you take Edward upstairs, Bella?"

"Because Grandmama said we should sit in the hallway."

Maya walked into the kitchen, where Grandmama and the younger aunts were eating Chinese food.

Aunt Linda had come in with Maya and asked Grandmama, "Did my daddy leave any money for me?"

Grandmama asked her in return, "What time is your mother coming home from work?" That was the only answer to Maya's question.

Mama was working at a small novelty store at the time, much like the five and dime off St. Charles Avenue.

"She's getting off at seven," Maya said. "She has to close tonight."

"Well." Grandmama sighed as she put her fork down and turned to Maya. "The Chinese store doesn't close till ten o'clock. She'll buy you kids a box of rice when she gets home."

Maya turned on her heels and told us to come upstairs with her now. We didn't have to sit there while they ate. Maya hated to babysit. Those kinds of things happened all the time. I knew that Maya wouldn't take it out on us, but she would take it out on Mama. I wanted to cry, remembering my sister's hidden resentment.

The groundskeeper's voice broke my inner thoughts. I looked at my sister again and saw what I thought were tears. We thanked the nice man, and he gave us his condolence and dropped us at the front steps of the main office. As I started to climb the stairs, Maya said, "Bella, I don't think Cicely wants to meet."

"What about you, Maya? What are you thinking?"

"We need to come together. Why?"

I started for the door as Cicely pushed her way out. "Come on, sis. Let's ride. What's up? You saw the place where Mama's going to be laid to rest?"

"Yeah," Maya said. "I rode over with you before, but we are all going to ride over."

Once again we climbed into our cars and started toward the site we had just left. The cars pulled up to the curb by the young tree. It felt like a small funeral rehearsal with just the six of us attending. We climbed out of our cars and headed down the little hill to the final resting place. We stood in silent awe.

Maya spoke. "That money has to be paid before they will open the ground."

Maya turned, and Cicely remarked, "Yeah," following Maya back to her car.

"Okay, we can do that. I'll see you back at Mama's," Edward said as he turned to go back to the car.

"Mama's house?" Cicely asked. "You mean my house." That wasn't the first clue. Cicely had the will, and she had no problem letting us know who was in charge. Maya told her to be quiet.

The ride to Mama's was quiet. We all heard what Cicely had just said. I didn't want to be the one to ask. I just wanted some healing between us.

The car turned onto Burgundy Street to St. Charles. Cicely's car was not there. They had left before us. As Edward was parking the car, Cicely pulled up behind him. We all went into the house and headed for the kitchen—except for Cicely, who headed straight for the basement.

We stood around in the kitchen, not talking. Taking all of us into consideration, just maybe we could share something that would bring us together. But we were acting like strangers in a waiting room. What were Mama's last wishes? If there had been a will or whatever to get us talking—whether we fixed our relationships with each other or not—was not of importance to me now.

"Maya, could we get started talking about how we are going to cover the cost of opening the ground?" We figure it would be $220 divided six ways."

Maya spoke with an icy tone. "Tony doesn't have money. He has a problem, right, Tony?" She flashed him a dirty look.

"I'm taking care of that, sis," Tony said. We all knew what Tony had been dealing with.

Lip threw a hundred on the kitchen table and said, "This is all the money I have."

Edward said, "I can make up the difference."

"I will, as well," I said.

"What is Cicely doing?" We all looked at Maya for the answer.

"What?" Maya asked, as if she was saying, *How dare you!* "Where" is Cicely?"

"What is she doing downstairs?" I asked.

Maya was becoming agitated and didn't want to answer. I got up from my seat and went to the basement door. "Cicely," I called, "we are waiting for you. Can you please come upstairs?"

After a while Cicely came into the kitchen and stood in the middle of the floor. "What? I don't want to meet with anybody. I'm busy trying to bury my mother."

"Cicely, she was our mama too."

I asked "Maya, for no other reason than for us to grieve in private."

"Maya never said what Mama's last wishes were. We need closure. We should be able to ask whatever questions concern our mama. Cicely, why won't you talk to us? We are all her children."

"Girl, who are you talking to?" Cicely asked as she came through the door into the kitchen. "You better leave me alone."

Cicely and Maya hadn't wanted to share anything about what was going on. Why?

Cicely walked over to the phone on the kitchen wall and started dialing a number.

Maya sat there staring into open space, not saying a word, like the rest of us. Cicely began to have an open conversation with the person on the other end of the line. "What are you doing? You know I'm doing my best to bury Mama, and Bella's here asking me questions about her mama's funeral."

"Who are you talking to, Cicely?" Lip asked.

"I'm talking to my son. They need to just fall back. Mama told me if anyone gives me any problems it would be Bella," Cicely shouted as she continued the conversation with her son. "That's what she told me, that you would be the problem if there was one."

Lip asked Cicely for the phone so he could speak with her son. "Look," Lip said, "we are here at Mama's house talking. I don't know why your mama has called you." Lip was listening, and then he told Cicely's son, "You might feel like Granny was your mama, but she wasn't. She was your grandmother." The conversation went somewhere else, and Lip got upset by Cicely's son's remarks.

Lip handed the phone back to Cicely. "Your son is wrong," Lip said. "You need to deal with your sisters and brothers."

Cicely yelled, "My son is my backbone now that my mama's gone!" Cicely hung up the phone and went into Mama's bedroom. She called Maya, but she didn't get up from the chair in which she was sitting."

"Cicely," I called from the kitchen, "Mama said she left a message in the Bible for us, so can I please see the Bible?"

Cicely came out of Mama's bedroom and stood over me. "You can't see anything," and Mama said, "You were something." "I told you, and if you don't leave me alone!" Girl! "The way I'm feeling."

Cicely approached me and stood over me as I sat at the table, across from Maya. "I'm not playing. We can fight now, 'cause it's been a long time coming, and I still can give you an ass whopping!" Cicely was getting closer to my face. She had been saving this rage. "Bella, you aren't anybody."

"Miss Bossy?" Edward asked Cicely. "Why are you acting like this?"

"I don't have to tell her anything. And you either when it's all said or done." Cicely shook her finger in Edward's face and said, "My sister and I are taking care of the business of burying *my* mama."

Maya finally told her to get out of my face. Lip got between us.

I stood up and left the house. Maya later came out of the house and handed me some papers while I sat in the car, waiting for Edward and Lip to take me to my daughter Danielle's house. The papers were Mama's will and the quick claim deed to the house. I didn't thank her, nor did I look at her. Maya put the papers in my lap and walked back into the house. I wanted to scream at the top of my lungs. But as I felt the hot tears roll down my face onto the papers that laid there, I could only whisper to myself, "This too shall pass."

Edward came and got into the car. "Want to go back to Danielle's or back in the house?"

"Why go back in there?" I asked, reading the will Maya had given me. "Please just take me to Danielle's house, Edward." I didn't want to go to the wake that night, and I sure didn't want to go to the funeral tomorrow.

When Edward dropped me off at my daughter's, my youngest daughter, Cholet, was there with her three children. I grabbed and hugged them, kissing them all over. They always made my soul happy when it was weary. My stories always made them happy. They were like a song of joy. "My brown sugar babies." Cholet was the mirror image of my mama. She was tall like my mama, all legs. Cholet had beautiful brown skin and long wavy hair. "How is everyone?" I managed to smile.

Cholet was in the living room on the sofa, with her knees to her chest. The energy was being sucked out of her. She was not the adventurous young mother who I had driven to Louisiana a year ago. Cholet was in a very bad relationship, and the effect of the abuse was starting to show. She was looking much older than her young twenty-five years. I knew she was still in some form of love, but I was hoping that she was done this time.

# Chapter Twelve
# Mama's Wake

I played with the kids for a while and then had something to eat. I didn't want to tell Danielle what had transpired at Mama's house. The phone rang, and I could hear Danielle was saying, "What? No sir. What! My mama hasn't said a word. Okay, talk with you later, girl. Yes, I'm going to the wake."

I could tell from the conversation that Zoe had been told what happened at Mama's house. "Who told"? I asked. "Nothing in this family can be kept where it lay. It was only us there, my sisters and brothers."

"What happened at Mama's house?" Danielle came and stood in front of me. "Mommy, what happened at Granny's house? Did Aunt Cicely want to fight you? Why didn't you say something when you got here?"

The questions were coming too fast for me to answer. "Danielle, can you please ask one question at a time? Well, I can say this. Aunt Cicely hasn't changed much."

"Why would she want to fight you?" Danielle asked with anger that gave me pause.

Cholet chimed in, expressing her view. "Jealousy! That's all this is. Jealousy. Because they know how much you have done for Granny, and they say all the time you are too bossy and think you know it all."

"So what!" Danielle shouted. "Aunt Cicely should be ashamed of the way she's acting."

I didn't want to talk about it. I didn't want to cry. I took a deep breath. I just wanted to go home, pack my bags, leave here, and never come back.

"Mommy, what happened?" she asked again.

I finally told what happened about my asking to meet with my sisters and brothers to discuss Mama.

"What did Aunt Maya do? Did she say anything?"

The questions started to fly again.

"Danielle, it was as if I was in a dream. I thought that we needed to sit together to clear the air between us and come together before we had to face the rest of the family, but Cicely didn't want to. So she did the only thing she knows how to: fight. She wanted to do whatever to not have us meet. But your aunt Maya brought me the will and power of attorney after I left the house and got into the car."

"Mommy, what would you have done if she hit you?"

"I don't know," I said. "I just don't know." I didn't have answers for anything right now.

Cholet was my focus at the moment. I wanted Cholet and her kids to come back to New York until she could get herself together. Cholet really didn't want to leave the relationship. She was in denial. The last time my mama had seen Cholet, she and the kids went to the nursing home to visit. My girls did that often. Mama had told Cholet to stop smoking and to pay close attention to her oldest daughter, to keep her close. Cholet was pregnant for the third time and didn't know she was until Mama told her on one of her visits to the nursing home. "Cholet, you are the fish I caught in my dream," she said in a raspy voice. Mama was having a hard time talking now that she had the surgery. But if Mama said something, it was good advice.

I looked at Cholet and asked her to please consider coming back to New York after the funeral.

"Mommy, I don't know."

"Go," Danielle said. "You need help right now, Cholet."

Cholet shot a look at Danielle. I could see that they were not getting along. I wanted to go to bed. The wake was at seven in the evening. It was still early, and Zoe hadn't returned from visiting her friends at the hotel, where she had worked at the time. Mama was finding it hard to pay the mortgage because of the loan, so Zoe moved in, but Cicely had also moved back home.

There had been a lot of tension when she came back. Zoe had moved into her old room, so Cicely complained so much until Zoe moved into Granny's bedroom.

"Mommy," Cholet called from the kitchen, "the kids and I are going to leave. We will see you at the wake tonight. Love you."

Danielle started to fix me a plate. She had cooked my favorite meal. She always did whenever I came home to visit. This time was no different. I wasn't very hungry, but I ate what I could.

Danielle poured me a glass of wine as we talked about what happened and how I was going to get through the wake and funeral. "I just want this over at this point. I don't want to go to the wake."

"Ma, you have done nothing wrong by wanting answers. I think Aunt Maya is behind Aunt Cicely's behavior."

"No, Danielle, your aunt has power of attorney. She gave me a copy of the will and the quick claim deed."

"How did Aunt Maya get power of attorney? When she did she see a lawyer?" Danielle was shouting. "She never went to the hospital, and she only went twice to the nursing home to see about Granny."

I forced myself out of the conversation. I was bewildered. I wanted to focus on tomorrow and how I wanted things to go. I tried to think about only the good, a time when life was easy and Mama was alive and well. That's what I wanted to think about.

I did not want to think about what could happen, after what already happened at Mama's house earlier. I closed my eyes and fell asleep, dreaming I was back on Esplanade Avenue. I was lying in the bunk bed in the living room. Cicely and I shared the top bunk. I was at the head of the bed, and Cicely was at the foot of the bed. Then there was this horrible pain that surged through my vaginal area. Cicely had kicked me as hard as she could. I yelled out, "Get your feet off me! Don't touch me." She had almost kicked me off the top bunk. "Mama! Cicely just kicked me in my privates."

"Cicely! Cicely, girl, you better answer me. Did you kick her?"

"I shoved her with my foot. I didn't kick her!"

Mama didn't get up to see if I was hurt.

The next morning I could hardly get down from the bunk because of the pain. I was bruised and solemn. Mama was cooking oatmeal when I came into the kitchen crying. I was in pain and could hardly walk. Mama said nothing about what had happened. I felt removed, as if someone else was having this dream. What was bothering me? I woke with dread. It was going on four in the morning, and I couldn't sleep. Why was I dreaming about Cicely and me? What was the reason I was waking up with memories that had been so hurtful to me? I could feel the pain down there now. That shit between Cicely and me at Mama's should not have happened. It felt good to be angry but what did it solve? Was I upset? Did I do something that caused Cicely to want a fight? I felt pain in my vaginal area. I felt that kick of so many years ago. I woke feeling tired and restless.

Danielle told me my brother would spend the night at one of his children's house. He would meet me at the hotel after the wake. I told her, "Okay, that's good I don't have to pick him up from God knows where."

I showered and went back to bed. Sleep came easy. The phone rang. "Who is it, honey?"

"It's Uncle Edward."

"Hello."

"Hey, sis, how are you feeling?"

"I'm okay. What about you?"

"I'm getting ready for the wake tonight. I heard none of Mama's friends have been notified about the funeral."

"Well, I'll talk to you tonight, okay?"

## Closing Chapter

"Okay, sis, I'll see you tonight."

I got up, fixed myself a cup of tea, and sat at the kitchen table. I pulled out my tarot cards to do a reading concerning the day's events. I wanted to be aware of any negative feelings that I may be carrying in my subconscious. "Danielle, did Maya or Cicely call yet?"

"No, Mommy, not yet, but don't wait for a call. They don't want you to know what Granny left in her will."

"I know, but should I care about those things?"

"Yes, you should, Mommy. She was your mother too."

Danielle looked wide-eyed. "Mommy, do you realize what you've done for your mother? How you have been there? Your sisters have not done half of what you've done, and you don't live here in Louisiana. You showed your mother love while she was living, so you have every right to question their actions."

"I feel that way sometimes," I said, "but could I have done more? I answered the call. If there was anything that Mama needed, I saw to it that she had it, whatever it was. I even paid the mortgage when Cicely was working and living there with her. If I could only tell them how many times Mama called me, complaining about the two of them. Mama would be crying about how Cicely was very mean to her. She talked to her as if she didn't care. She would refer to her as the old lady when I called. Cicely said Mama was getting on her nerves with her sickness, and she wanted to move to Atlanta with her son. I told her to go if that was what she wanted. I do believe Mama never forgave me for that encouragement that I gave Cicely."

The truth is Cicely was not helping Mama. She was more of a burden to her, as was Maya, after they lost their house and had nowhere to go. Mama was Maya's saving grace. I knew this because Mama told me these things from her own lips. These thoughts ran through my mind as Danielle told me not to be focus on Maya's or Cicely's behavior anymore and just get through the next two days.

I decided to take a long bubble bath, even though I had taken a shower that morning. I needed to meditate after my reading. I wanted my mind at rest and my heart at peace. I needed spiritual, emotional, and mental security. My intuition was in high vibration, and I needed to find the emotion to fit that.

What did I need to know? I didn't want to be right. I just wanted to release years of resistance.

"What time is it?"

"Three o'clock," my granddaughter yelled from the living room.

I was pouring myself another cup of tea. There are some things for which we have to forgive ourselves, but there are other things for which we never seek forgiveness because we don't ask.

"Granny, your bubble bath is ready."

"Thank you, sweetheart."

The bath was inviting, and the bubbles soothed my soul as I sank into them. I closed my eyes and was reminded that sometimes I had to distance myself from everything and everybody. I had to find that space for a moment of silence.

I wondered if Mama's sisters and brothers were heartbroken. Did they grieve? These questions went unanswered. Had they endured since hearing the news? Mama was the head of the family, yet the family for most of us without my mother's support and that made it function, now lost and greatly divided. Where was appreciation? A few of my aunts loved my mother dearly and would do anything for Rachel. I thanked God for Beverly and Cookie. I longed to express this love for them all. But I was still learning. The heat from the bubble bath was making me relax. I began to breathe in the quiet and release the tension. My breathing was calming.

"Ma, telephone!" Danielle yelled.

"Who is it? I'll be out in a second. Can you take a message, honey?"

"Uncle Philip wants to know what time you are going to the wake. They want all the children there early before the rest of the family arrives."

"Tell your uncle I guess around 6:30 p.m."

I told Lisa I would come over to her house and then go to the club. It was getting near time to get dressed, but I wasn't in any hurry. Zoe had just gotten back from the hotel, and she was still quite lost in her own world. Zoe had certainly had her share of disappointments and setbacks, but I guess you learn who you really are by the way you embrace life. She was giving voice to her granny's death. Cicely lost her father, who she loved unconditionally. Larry was never fully in her life until she became a woman and then because she was trying to get him off drugs.

I asked Danielle to pour me a glass of wine. I wanted to talk to my daughters about what had happened at Mama's. "I know I have nothing to apologize for, but I want you girls to know that I did the best I could for you. You are all each other has, and it's never too late to hone your positive outlook and love of each other. Learn to gratify each other. Be committed to family."

"Ma, we could never treat each other the way your sisters are treating you." Danielle and Zoe both said the same thing at the same time.

I laughed. "You girls make a wish. Make it come true for me and my sisters and brothers, as well."

"Good to see you laugh, Granny," Matthew said as he came busting in the kitchen door, carrying an armful of Chinese food. "Mommy, eat something before you get dressed. You have plenty of time."

We all ate and had some good conversation. I was there physically but mentally preoccupied. My estrangement from my sisters and brothers was tough. Their expectations would change now that Mama was gone, and maybe their expectations were the shadows in front of their reality.

We arrived at 6:25 p.m. When we entered the funeral home for the wake, Maya, Cicely, and Tony were already there. Neither Philip nor Edward had arrived. I didn't know if I should embrace them or not. They made it easy for me by walking straight into the room where the wake was to be held. There was Cicely in her workhouse uniform, with her coworkers in tow, just like the church sisters. They all gathered around Mama, who was lying in her coffin. Maya sat in the front row and looked straight ahead. As I was making my way to the front of the room, Edward called out to me.

I turned around to see Eddie and his oldest daughters, Karen and Connie. "Hi, Aunt Bella. You okay?"

"I'm fine. Thank you, honey. How are you ladies?"

I didn't expect Connie and Karen to really be in tears over my mother. But they were. There hadn't been a grandmother–granddaughter relationship for a long time. I had been gone awhile, so a lot of the details surrounding Edward and Mama were pretty much Mama's version of events.

On Christmas Mama would buy all the grandchildren gifts. She had done so for many years, and Edward never brought his, so after a time Mama told me she stopped buying for his girls. He wouldn't even pick up the presents after Christmas. Well, one Christmas Edward and his family just showed up, and Mama had no gifts for his girls.

Connie never forgot this unkind act. Connie told my daughter Danielle about it many years later, after she found out that Mama was sick and had called for a family meeting, which her father never told her about. She didn't want to come to Granny's house, because she didn't like the way Granny allowed Cicely to talk to her kids when it wasn't Cicely's house. Connie wasn't the only grandchild who confessed that she held some anger or hurt feelings that were caused by Mama.

Maya's daughters became distanced when Mama said things about their father, which Maya didn't like. She stayed away and, therefore, so did her children. Mama called me and told me that Maya had gotten upset because she didn't appreciate Mama accusing Carl, Maya's husband, of charging her to cash her social security check.

Mama was more upset that Maya couldn't understand her feelings about what was going on. I got to see for myself what Mama had meant. All things were made clear with time. Mama wanted Maya to defend her position about the check and being charged. Time changed my sister's world, and Mama watched it all crumble. She called me when Maya and Carl lost their house. They had fallen on hard times. Did Mama call to gloat?

By eight at night, everyone was in attendance. I moved from the front of the room to the back and sat with Cholet and the kids. Family and friends filed in. There was lots of laughter from those who hadn't seen each other in some time. I hadn't seen most of them since I had given the cookout at Mama's on one of my visits.

Edward and I decided that it would be good for Mama to see the family, as she had been complaining that she didn't feel that she was going to be with us much longer. It turned out wonderful. Everyone showed but Aunt Linda. The night was still early. Maybe she would still come. Cicely had invited most of her coworkers, and they behaved as if they were at a meet and greet, talking loudly and drawing attention to themselves. It looked like a social gathering.

My great-aunt Agatha Ann, who was Mama's closest friend and only aunt, sat next to me and whispered, "You're going to miss your mama, huh?"

I didn't want to speak, for I knew if I answered I would cry. I was not going to do that!

"How come you're not sitting up front with your sisters?"

"I don't know. I just wanted to sit here with the kids."

"Oh, these are your grandkids? Who do they belong to?"

"Cholet," I said, not making eye contact.

Aunt Agatha Ann had no idea what happened at Mama's house earlier. I didn't want to be anywhere near Cicely or Maya.

"Hey, Agatha Ann," Aunt Ellie said as she spotted her talking to me in the back of the room. Most had gathered around the front near Mama's casket.

"How are you doing, girl?"

"It's been a long time. How is everyone?" Aunt Ellie asked Great-Aunt Agatha Ann. "I just saw Mel. Girl, your son has put on some pounds."

"I know," said Aunt Agatha Ann. "Since he moved back home, all he does is eat."

Aunt Ellie was going on nonstop. They both broke out in laughter.

"Excuse me, girl, I'm talking to my great-niece. I haven't seen her in such a long time."

Aunt Agatha Ann took me by the arm and walked me to the front. We stopped at Mama's casket. As we stood there, she made a comment that tore through me. "Your sisters have had a hard time taking care of your mother. Now they will have peace."

My stomach hurt. "I need to go to the ladies room, Aunt Agatha." Where was this information coming from? They took care of Mama! They put her in the damn nursing home! There was a war going on in my mind. I was bitter.

Maya and Cicely could have done much more for Mama. The two of them waiting for mama's death I stood in the ladies room, looking in the mirror. I needed to resist the thoughts that were condemning.

"Cousin, are you okay?" It was Sandy.

"Sure, I'm all right, thanks. How are you?" I was more like an aunt to Sandy than a cousin because of our age. We walked back into the room together.

"Bella, why didn't you come to my mother's funeral?"

*Huh? Where did that come from?* I looked at Sandy, and the only thing I could say was "Sorry that I wasn't there for you. I loved your mother, and you know that."

"I know, but I looked for you," Sandy said.

I didn't really have the heart to tell her that at the time Aunt Rose passed I was doing drugs. Sandy and her mother lived down the street from Mama. Before they moved to Orlando, Florida, I spent a many evenings at Aunt Rose's house. Aunt Rose had been my partner in crime when she worked at Lord and Taylor. She was a junior buyer. Aunt Rose would bring home clothing, and I would take orders from the girls at my job.

*Closing Chapter*

There was a lot of baggage that came with her life. Years earlier she had left her two children on Grandmama and Grandpapa's front porch one night and went to California. Aunt Rose died from cancer. Why did I have those memories? It was how I guess I measured. I smiled.

"Sandy, how are your children? I heard you were a grandmother."

"Yeah, my oldest daughter is here somewhere with her baby. How many grandchildren do you have now?" Sandy asked.

"Well, my daughter Danielle has the two, and Alex, my son, has two girls. My Cholet, who is my youngest, has three."

"Oh, wow, seven?" Sandy laughed.

"Yeah, girl." We both laughed. Sandy got up to go look for her daughter.

I heard a voice calling me. "Bella, come here for a minute, please." Aunt Tamar was standing near the front of the room with a female whom I recognized but couldn't name. "Do you remember who this is?"

"Yes, hi, Aunt Barbara." The name flowed from my lips, as if I had talked to Aunt Barbara just the other day. "How's Eric?" Eric was Uncle Miles's son. He and Barbara had been married but divorced after I moved away. They taught at the same school. The marriage didn't last, but she remained close with Mama. Aunt Barbara couldn't deal with Uncle Miles during the civil rights movement.

Uncle Miles had married three times, and all of his ex-wives were there. Uncle Miles was there with wife number four, Joyce. Mama loved them all dearly. Mama was always overprotective, which didn't make her well liked by most her sisters- and brothers-in-law. Mama loved you as long as you loved her sister or brother. After the love was gone, so was Mama's love for you. Mama loved that Uncle Miles's fourth wife, Joyce, who worked at the Employment Services, got her baby brother a job when he was released from prison. Joyce even got Maya's husband a job there too.

Uncle Brother, the oldest of Mama's four brothers, attended the wake. Uncle Paul Jr. walked slower and had a distant look in his eyes. He hadn't been well, and Aunt Ella had retired so she could be his caregiver. Aunt Ella was a schoolteacher. They went everywhere together except to Mama's house. Mama always said, "Aunt Ella could drop him off to visit." But she didn't because she didn't really like her.

Mama never really told me what happened between them. She only said that Aunt Agatha and Aunt Ella had gotten close, because Mama couldn't travel anymore. They were always traveling when Mama was well. Now that Mama had gotten sick and could no longer go with them, she became bitter at whoever she thought was at fault.

"Excuse me, Aunt Barbara," I said. "I want to speak to my aunt and uncle."

"You take care, Bella, and I hope we see each other again under different circumstances."

I kissed her on the cheek and left her and Aunt Tamar standing there. My thoughts were somewhere else.

I sat there in the back row and looked around the room for Danielle and Zoe.

"Who are you looking for?" I turned. Ruth was standing there in tears, holding her arms out to me. "Oh, Bella, I'm going to miss your mama so much. I hadn't seen Reese in a long time."

Reese was Mama's nickname. My mama's brothers mainly called her Black, but most of the younger members in the family called her Reese. Everyone who I talked to was referring to Mama as "your mother." It was good to hear her nickname. I hugged Ruth. She was the first person I embraced and the second whom I saw cry.

"I love you too."

"I know you loved my mother."

"Oh, Bella, when I heard the news I cried all day. I couldn't go to work. I'm so sorry that I didn't visit Reese more at the nursing home. I thought I had more time." Her tears were warm as she pulled her face close to mine.

"Ruth, I understand you."

"I miss her, Bella." She sobbed.

Mama had let Ruth come live with her after she graduated from the eighth grade. She was going into high school. Aunt Barbara, Mama's sister and Ruth's mother, had emotional problems, and things had been unstable for quite some time after her son Kenneth's death. Ruth needed to be away from the drama, so she moved in with Mama. I also had moved home during that time. So we talked about life and what she wanted to do when she graduated from high school. Ruth wanted to become a nurse, and she did. Her mother had died a couple of years before Grandmama, so she knew how I was feeling at that moment.

"I'm glad you and your family are doing okay, girl."

"They are." I smiled.

"I'm a grandmama now too," she said. We both laughed softly in each other's ear. "Love you, Bella."

"Love you, Ruth."

I spoke to my uncle Wilbert, who was sitting with his wife, Aunt Jean, and his daughter, Candia. Uncle Wilbert's story about his runaway son could be told at its best by only Mama. No one had heard a word from him. Mama would get upset with Uncle Wilbert, because he didn't try to find him. No one knew where he had gone. He could be dead. Mama never gave him any peace, so Uncle Wilbert wouldn't come over as much. Mama blamed Uncle Wilbert. He should love him regardless of his lifestyle.

The room became crowded, and noise swirled in my head. I got up and stepped just outside the room. Maya was talking with her husband, Carl. She had been complaining that she was ready to leave. I had given Maya the two hundred dollars, which was my share of the money to break the ground. She had been collecting envelopes from the guests. Now she was ready to leave. It was getting late, and I was ready to leave.

Lisa caught me as I was getting my coat and looking for my daughters. "Bella, I've been looking for you."

"Come on, Zoe, outside with Danielle."

"I want to know if you all are going to the wake party." It was nine thirty, and there were plenty people left inside.

"Who else is going?" I asked.

"My sister and mother are coming, so come on, Bella. You need to release some of your sorrow and spend some time with your family."

I didn't know what I wanted to do. I stood there in the night air and looked around as people were leaving and bidding long good-byes and hugs to those whom they knew they wouldn't see again. Many who attended the wake would not be attending the funeral tomorrow. I was lost in the moment. The cold was chilling. I wrapped my coat tight around my body and sighed. Well, I made it. No words had passed between my sisters and me. I didn't know if anyone had noticed the distance that I had put between them and me.

"Hey, Bella, what's up? I didn't get a chance to say anything to you. How are you?" Peaches had been a family friend for many years. She was always with my aunt Linda and Maya. They did everything together.

"Peaches, I'm all right. I saw your brother, Red Boy, and your sister, Alexis, inside. Thanks for coming," I said as I gave her a hug.

"Times have changed, huh?"

"Yeah, they have, Peaches."

"I guess so. We are getting a little wiser. Where is your aunt Linda?"

"I don't know. You are her are best friend. Don't you know?"

"Girl, I haven't seen your aunt since the last family reunion."

"Peaches, we haven't had a family reunion since Mama was sick."

"Yeah, your mother was responsible for all the family gatherings, huh?"

"Mostly, yes."

"You live on the East Coast now, don't you?"

"I do. I have been living in Harlem over thirty years, and I've seen many changes there, as well as at home."

"Wow! Girl, you've been gone now longer than you have lived at home, huh?"

"I know it doesn't feel like I've be gone that long, but I have."

"You didn't see your mother much when she got sick, did you?"

"Peaches, I came home as much as I could, every three months when my mama went to the nursing home."

"I didn't know Reese was in a nursing home, girl. Maya never told me that."

"Mama had been in the nursing home for two years, Peaches."

"Oh my God. As much as I talked with Maya, she never said a word about your mother."

"Come on, Mommy. We're leaving. Let's go." Danielle was heading for the car, and the parking lot was emptying.

"Peaches, I have to go."

"Bella, I'll see you tomorrow, okay?"

"Okay." I walked toward the car and looked back, remembering my mama lying in the casket alone and maybe not so much at rest.

"What a night!" Lisa shouted to us from across the parking lot.

"You know the way to the club?"

"Yeah," Danielle said. "We'll see you in a few." The cars were now pulling into the parking lot at Zimmer's Club. "Ma, I don't want you to be here too late. The funeral is at ten in the morning. Okay?"

"Danielle, where is Zoe?" I asked

"Oh, she rode with Uncle Philip. They went to the hotel."

Zoe didn't want to come for drinks. She was still upset with Maya and Cicely. As we entered the club, Linda grabbed and hugged me. "We love you, Bella!"

"Yes, we do," said Aunt Ellie as she put her arms around me for a group hug.

Lisa came over, and we all stood there embracing each other.

Aunt Ellie had come in with her two daughters, Lisa and Linda. They were twins. They both had just become mothers. Mama had called and told me the story. Aunt Ellie was upset with Linda because she had left her husband. Lisa had just gotten a divorce and was living at mama's house. There had been other things that tore at Mama and my aunt Ellie's relationship.

It was awful for Mama to be home after Aunt Ellie and Aunt Tamar put Grandpapa in a nursing home. Mama had gotten a lawyer and took them both to probate court. No one showed up but Uncle Miles and Uncle Wilbert. Mama was very disappointed at the rest of her sisters and brothers who didn't make the effort to do so. Aunt Tamar never cared about what happened on Esplanade Avenue or about anybody who lived in the house. Aunt Tamar had taken control, with no regard for those who still needed shelter. Most of the family had begun to show at the club.

Peaches came in with Aunt Linda, who I had not seen since I moved to New York. She had gotten older, but the years had been kind. We held each other for quite a while. I allowed the energy between us to melt into warm love. She whispered into my ear, "I will not be at the funeral tomorrow, okay?"

I shook my head. She needed to say no more. I was just happy to see her.

Uncle Miles had begged her to give him his father's guns and old coins, but she refused. I let the music bring me back from the memories that reminded me so much of the situation with my sisters and the part that Aunt Tamar played in putting my mother in that awful nursing home where she lay and died.

"Sure, make mine a glass of white wine."

The waitress took everyone else's order. I took a sip of my drink as I let the music soothe my mind and relax my nerves.

"Aunt Ellie, is that the charm bracelet I gave to my mother?"

"Yes, Bella, your sister gave it to me."

"What?" I asked.

"Cicely gave it to me the day your mother died."

I was heartbroken. Aunt Ellie turned away from me and adjusted her seat, so as not to be as close. But I told Aunt Ellie I bought that for my mother.

"Cicely gave me this, honey."

I wasn't expecting that for an answer. The atmosphere changed, and we both felt it. Aunt Ellie knew I didn't have a problem speaking up, but I held my peace.

"Aunt Ellie, what else did Cicely give you that was my mother's?"

"Oh, honey, we don't need to talk about those things now, do we?"

But I asked another question. "Is that the coat I bought my mama?"

"Are you talking about this one?"

"Yes, that one. I brought that coat for my mother and the one Maya wore to the wake. I bought both for her. I brought Mama something every time I came to visit. I would buy her clothes, jewelry, and figurines." I beckoned for the waitress to come over to the table. I ordered myself another wine and asked my aunt what she was drinking.

"Nothing. I have to get ready for tomorrow. Did you bring any smoke with you?"

"No, I didn't bring any to the wake, Aunt Ellie."

"I didn't think you were high at your mother's wake. I didn't know what to expect from you, Bella. You were acting strange at the wake, so I didn't want to bother you. I thought maybe you were a little high."

"No, my mother had just died."

Aunt Ellie finished her drink. "Let Lisa and Linda know I'm gone." Aunt Ellie got up and headed for the door. I watched as she disappeared into the darkness.

Lisa and Linda were busy burning up the dance floor. Left alone, I nursed my glass of wine as I watched my family wild away the night. I remembered when I used to dance the night away. My family knew how to have a good time. I smiled to myself and even laughed a little out loud. My family's love was bittersweet, but to leave them in my past was all too impossible. They were mine, and I loved them most of the time.

Lisa dropped in her seat. "Boy, that was a long record. What are you drinking?"

"White wine," I said as I looked to see if Danielle was getting off the dance floor. She was still going strong. "Aunt Ellie said she had to go."

"Really? How long ago did she leave?"

"Oh, she just left."

The music stopped for a minute as the DJ's voice broke in. He announced that a beautiful person had just left the company of this world, that she had an appointment in heaven, and that her family was there to send her off with dance and drink. "So let's all raise our glasses and drink to Rachel Thurston. We will surely miss you."

I raised my glass and said, "This one's for you, Mama." I drank it down and asked for another. When the second drink came, I drank it down too. Danielle finally came off the dance floor, and by this time the wine was now taking effect. "Well, hi, baby. Did you shake a tail feather or what?"

"Yes, I did. What are you drinking?"

"I just finished off my third glass of wine."

"Mommy's buzzed."

I asked Danielle, "Are you going to have a drink?"

Danielle took a napkin and wiped the sweat from her face. "Yeah, if you don't mind, Mommy."

"Okay, I'm going to the ladies room." I had not done much to fill this empty space that had been with me since Cicely called me.

Everything that came after it only deepened the sadness that now wouldn't leave me. I found myself looking in the mirror with different eyes. I was crying my heart out, but not a tear had fallen from my eyes.

"Hey, Bella!" Lark grabbed me as she came into the ladies room. Lark was my aunt Carmen's daughter. Lark was always loud, and she could uplift you with her who-gives-a-damn attitude. "Girl, I know you're going to miss your mama, 'cause I'm missing her already. Bella, your mama was good to me. She bailed me out of jail, you know. I know you know how much she did for me and my kids. Now, girl, I got to go for the straight and narrow 'cause your mama's not going to be here to help a sister out. Bella," she went on as she came out of the stall, "my mama just cried her heart out, saying over and over, 'My sister's gone. My sister's gone.'"

"I know, Lark. We all are going to miss my mother, and she was there for us all. Let me get going, girl, and I'll see you tomorrow."

As I swung the door back, she yelled that "you will"

I laughed. Who was it that said pain and sorrow come from the same place but rarely do they sit down together? I thought if that was so, then when I laughed, the sorrow would be gone in that moment. If only I could find the humor in my mother's death, then I could make it through the funeral with flying colors. That was not that a joke. I smiled to myself again. *This stuff really works.*

"Ma, you ready to go?" Danielle asked when I made my way back to our table.

"Sure, I feel a lot better now, sweetheart. Let's go."

As we made our way into the night traffic, Danielle turned on the car radio to a blues station. Etta James was crying out one of her hits from the late fifties. It took me back to the kitchen upstairs on Esplanade Avenue. Mama was doing Aunt Rose's hair. Aunt Rose had high hopes of becoming a singer and dancer, so she would go to amateur night at the local nightclub in East Louisiana. She and her girlfriend Addie Mae were going to grow up and be famous. Etta James was singing about how her love had come along, and Aunt Rose was trying to tell Mama about how her ticket to Hollywood and stardom also had come along. As the song ended, so did the memory.

"Ma, you want to get something to eat before you go to the hotel?" Danielle was pulling into the hotel parking garage.

"No, I'll order room service in the morning." I collected the key and went to the room.

Philip was still awake when I came into the room. "What's up, sis?"

"Hey," I answered. "Nothing much. You didn't make it over to the club, huh? The family did a farewell to Mama, and we all toasted her life. I got a little buzzed, but nothing serious."

"Bella, what are we going to do about Mama's will?"

"I don't know, Philip."

"Well, is Maya going to read the will?"

"If you want, Philip, you can read what Maya gave me." I pulled the papers out of my carrying bag and handed them to Philip. He sat and read them while I took a shower and put on my pajamas. As I came out of the bathroom, Philip was just finishing up the last pages of the will. I waited for him to speak.

"Bella, what I get from what I read is that Mama wanted her kids to share what she left. Did you get that when you read it?"

"Really, Philip, I would need to have a lawyer look at it. But I will say this: the quick claim deed was done right before Mama went into the nursing home, so I think Mama gave up when she came home, thinking everyone that took the class was going to care for her."

"How do you know that?"

"Well, I got a call from the rehabilitation hospital. The lady I spoke with told me that it was time for Mama to be released and they—being Edward, Cicely, and Tony—they all took the training and were going to care for Mama at home. I was told that they were not making the necessary arrangements. The release date was now past due. They needed to arrange for medical equipment and a nurse. None of this had been done. So I made arrangements for the medical equipment, and I spoke with two of the nurses that work at the hospital. Now, Philip, when I called Cicely and told her most of what they needed to get Mama home, I gave her the numbers. I had spoken with these two nurses at the hospital and had Danielle interview them.

"What do you mean?" Philip asked. "You had Danielle interview the nurses?"

"Yeah. Philip, Danielle went to the hospital every day when Mama was a patient."

"Oh, really?" Philip didn't know a lot about what was going on with Mama before she went into the nursing home.

"Well, anyway, I didn't want to go into everything that transpired, like you can imagine. But what I'm telling you is this wasn't until Mama came home that she signed the quick claim deed. Mama was home not even a month before she was back in the hospital. I believe she forgot that she even signed it, because she was sure that the nursing home was not an option. Listen, we can go over those papers at some other time. I need to get some sleep. I'll talk to you in the morning."

"Yeah, sis. It's 12:42 a.m. See you in the next few hours."

"Good night, Philip." I drifted off to sleep, thinking that I had made up my mind to confront Cicely and Maya, but I also knew that I had to go along with certain things. It was like the currents of the river rushing past the shore. I didn't want to fight. My breathing was slowing down, and my thoughts wandered off to the funeral tomorrow.

I was drawn to the front porch, standing beside Mama. Gangs of people gathered around the yard. Mama was shouting, "Who are you looking for? Why are all these people here?"

This tall dark girl, with her hands on her hips, spoke up and shouted back at my mama, "You tell Carmen to come on out here! She better bring her ass out here! She wants to talk about people? Let her back it up. Yeah, that's right!"

Christine from up the street said Mama knew her and her family because of the neighborhood grocery store that our family owned.

Everyone was screaming back and forth. Mama was ready to come off the porch. My mama thought of herself as the neighborhood peacemaker for all the fights that found their way to our front yard. But this time was different. We hadn't been on Esplanade Avenue for very long. Mama was short on patience lately. Mama shouted for Aunt Carmen to come outside to the front. Grandmama and my aunt Carmen came out to the front porch.

I felt myself tossing and turning in my sleep. I knew I was reliving this moment, but why? I could see Mama clearly turning to Aunt Carmen and telling her to go down there and beat her ass. "And if you don't, I'll be waiting up here on this porch to beat yours!"

Mama was mad, but there was that smile on her face, the one we knew so well. Everyone had come out on their porches too. Aunt Carmen started down the front stairs, and Mama was following close behind. The rest of us were behind Mama. "Get back on the porch," Grandmama said, using her hand to shove us back.

Aunt Carmen came face-to-face with the girl she didn't know, the one who had called her out. Aunt Carmen never spoke a word. She just started pounding on her. The crowd gathered. After what seemed like forever, Mama pulled Aunt Carmen off the girl, and then she said to her, "Now fight, Christine." No sooner had she said that than Aunt Carmen started pounding on her too!

Christine lived up the street. She had brought the new girl to the neighborhood. Christine's mother was one of the onlookers from her porch, and she started to shout for my mama to stop the fight. Mama yelled up the street, "You come down and stop it. Your daughter was the one who brought this crowd to my house." When Mama felt she had enough, she told Aunt Carmen, "Now you don't have to worry about who your friends are anymore."

It was as if I had turned a movie on and then off. I fell into a deep sleep.

Chapter Thirteen

# Mama's Funeral

The early-morning silence woke me, and there was this glow. I meditated in the moment and recalled what the dream meant. The dread that I had been feeling had nothing to do with how my mother was to be honored, but knowing she deserved honor and knew her worth. I lifted myself from the bed. It was 5:33 a.m. I reached for the phone and ordered room service. Philip was still in a deep sleep. He was breathing heavily and looked very much at peace—almost dead, if not for his breath. I tiptoed to the bathroom and ran a bath. We had plenty of time before we had to be at Mama's house. I had to stop saying "Mama's house." I knew that the phone number was still the same and the voice mail still had Mama's voice, but the house was no longer the home I knew.

The room service arrived, "Good morning, sleepyhead," I said and smiled. I wanted him to be okay. "I ordered breakfast if you want. I have some tea, and there is coffee."

"Well, sis, today's the day,"

"I know," I said as I went to the bathroom with my cup of tea. I was going to relax and have a hot bubble bath. The phone rang as I was laying out my clothes for the funeral. "Hello."

"Morning, Ma." It was Danielle.

"Good morning, honey."

"What time do you and Uncle Philip want to leave?"

"Well, if services start at ten o'clock, then nine fifteen is good. We'll get to Cicely's—"

Danielle intruded and said, "That's Granny's house, so we're going to Granny's."

"We'll be down in the lobby."

Danielle pulled up to the front of the hotel on time. "Did you speak to Zoe, Mommy?" Danielle asked as she exited the car.

"No, not yet."

"Well, she's on her way down. So are you all ready? How are you feeling, Uncle Philip?"

"Good." Philip walked outside to have a cigarette while we waited for Zoe to come down to the lobby.

"Good morning, everybody." Zoe was in a better mood than she was at the wake, and I was happy for that.

"Good morning, honey. How are you?"

"Oh, I'm good, Mommy." She was good at hiding her feelings.

"Are you ready to speak this morning?" I asked her as I gave a simile.

"Yeah, I am. I don't have any idea what I'm going to say, but I know I want to speak."

Each of the oldest grandchildren was to say a few words. I knew how that made Zoe feel. She had gone through a very troubling time when she stayed with Mama. We all knew that Mama's illness was not going to get any better. Zoe decided not to move to New York right away. Cicely had moved next door to Mama and was working. Maya had lost her house and had moved in with Cicely. Philip had moved back home. Tony was on the outs with his wife, who wanted a divorce, and Mama didn't want her to divorce him. This was during the time that Mama was once again bearing the weight of her family's problems. And Zoe was hearing her complaints day in and day out. There was so much that Zoe could speak about. Zoe returned her keys to the front desk.

"Come on. Let's get to Granny's."

We pulled up to the house. The mor[ning chill was in] the air, but the sun was strong. I drew i[n a deep breath.] December 8, 2005. The sun warmed me a[s I got out. I didn't] know what to expect. I made my way up [the stairs. This was the] last time all of us met at Mama's house, C[...]

Aunt Agatha came to the door and embrace[d me. "Are you] okay?"

"Sure, I'm fine." I joined Aunt Tamar and Uncle Nelson in the living room. Everyone else was running around, doing whatever. Danielle and Zoe had stayed out front on the porch with Cicely's boys. The limo was double-parked in front of the house.

Aunt Agatha called me into the kitchen. "I want to know if your family wants to ride in the limo with Cicely's boys."

"I ordered a second limo for her family."

"I need to ask them."

"Auntie," I said, "I knew they were not going to accept the ride, but I asked my daughters if they wanted to ride."

"No!" they said in unison.

Aunt Agatha said, "I'll give them a call."

"The limos should be out there. There was one when I came in, Aunt Agatha." I spoke to everyone who was in the kitchen. I turned to see my sisters coming out of Mama's bedroom. They, along with Aunt Ellie, were dressed in white and draped in Mama's jewelry. Aunt Ellie was wearing the charm bracelet. They decided to dress alike, and no one told me. And there I was, all dressed in black. We were not on the same page. I was again understudy; this was how the role was being played. Feeling was confirmed more than the Wake the night before. "Grab your coats, everybody. The second limo is outside!"

I began to mark the time. My sister Maya led the way in the light brown winter coat that I had bought Mama. Aunt Ellie had on the older white winter coat that I also had brought my mama. Had they already gone through all of Mama's personals belongings without the rest of us? How could they! I was upset

...nted to cry, not for Mama but for the moments out of ...h I had been cheated.

I couldn't describe my feelings. I couldn't find words to go with what I was feeling. I became numb. I put myself in a trance and just went through the motions. I couldn't speak, standing there on the front porch with my aunts Agatha and Tamar, my brothers and sisters, and my girls. I then noticed they cut down the trees that used to be in front of the lot. I hadn't noticed that before. Cicely's son Todd was directing his kids and family into the second limo. Carl, my brother-in-law, was helping Maya down the front stairs in front of everyone waiting on the porch. Zoe, who was walking behind me, whispered, "Mommy, Danielle and I are not riding in the limo. We'll see you at the church, okay?"

With a kiss I watched until she was across the street and got in the car with Danielle. I climbed into the limo with my sisters and brothers. Would this be the final ride together? When would we be all together like this again? I was drowning in my own tears that I was holding back. It was heartbreaking. My soul was consumed with sorrow from how we were treating ourselves. I was feeling sick, hurt, and disgusted. There was no room for closure. I just had to walk away. *Like your mother said, you did twenty years earlier.* I was now speaking in the second person. One of the many things Mama and I would argue about was why I had moved to New York. After all those years, she'd say I had abandoned her. *Now you're feeling abandoned, and you are blaming your sisters.* I took a deep breath. The being the light and dark side trying to blend together, but peace and sorrow rarely sat down together.

I sat in the corner, facing Edward and Tony at the other end of the limo. Philip, Carl, and Maya sat on the long seat in the middle. Cicely rode up front with the limo driver.

It wasn't at all what it seemed. I could see Cicely running the show, leading the parade. The inner voice wanted me to see something else, but I had my own perception of what was.

*Closing Chapter*

As the limo pulled into Union, Cicely pulled back the window that separated the driver from the passengers. "Maya, did you see the obituary?"

"Yeah, it looked nice."

They were just having a conversation. The voice rang in, telling me that I didn't need to know the details.

"Well, I didn't put it out yet. I have a box in the second limo, and I want to make sure our kids get one."

*See, you're making sure every one of Rachel Thurston's children gets one.* The voice in second person made it hard for me to argue. But it was hard to even focus on what was happening from one moment to the next.

Cicely kept the window open as she talked back and forth with Maya and the driver. We slowed down and idled for a while as the driver hopped out of the front seat to see what the problem was. He came back to the car and got in. Before he could get a word out, Cicely asked, "What's up? Why did we stop in the middle of the street like this? It looks like people are still going into the church, so we have to wait until everyone goes in."

"The preacher hasn't arrived yet. He informed us we'll be parked here for a while."

We sat in front of North Side Baptist and watched as family and friends greeted each other and went into the church. I saw Mrs. Parks and her family make their way up the church stairs. Mrs. Parks was always like an aunt. She was my childhood best friend LeAnn's aunt. We grew up together as children until LeAnn's death. They lived across the street from Grandpapa's grocery store. LeAnn's father didn't live at home like mine. He kept moving in and out. I was very grateful to have LeAnn's family in my life even after she died. My heart felt good to see them the night before. Just as I was thinking about them, Cicely said, "Bella, did you see the Parkses?" That was the first time Cicely had included me in her conversation since we were riding.

"No, but I saw Derek at the wake last night."

"Oh, really," Cicely said with a little laugh. There was laughter in the whole car, an unspoken joke I didn't get.

The driver opened the car door, and I got out and waited for everyone else. We entered the church to find most of the family standing right inside the door. Church members dressed in usher uniforms and white gloves came over to us and asked the children of Rachel Thurston, the deceased, to please form a line. We all lined up in the small crowded entrance. As the music began to play, the doors were swung open by two other church ladies in usher uniforms and white gloves.

All turned to watch as we were escorted by two churchmen in black suits down to the front of the church. It had been a while since I had been inside a house of worship. It was by choice that I had left the church. I was seated next to Maya and brother-in-law Carl. Edward sat to my right, Philip was next to Tony, and he was next to Cicely, who sat at the other end of the first row.

The church was quiet except for the music that was being softly played by a lone piano player. The pastor stood as a predator of young women in his congregation. I looked at him standing over my mother's casket, hoping he would make eye contact with me. The call had come from Danielle one evening, telling me that Chrystal had gone to the North Side Day Care, run by the church that Mama and the rest of the family attended. Aunt Ellie had found the North Side when she moved from Esplanade Avenue. She invited the rest of the family to visit.

My mama and Aunt Tamar were the only ones left at Burning Bush after Grandmama had died. Mama became a mother of this new church and loved the new pastor. After I got the story from Danielle, I hung up the phone and called Chrystal. "Hello, Chrystal. How are you and the kids?"

"I'm good, the kids bad, Auntie!" She was laughing. "You know how kids are. As long as they're not sick, it's all good."

I laughed too. "Danielle called me." I paused. "Tell me what happened today."

"Aunt Bella, I went to pick up the kids over at the church's day care, and the minister approached me, like 'How are you doing?'"

"Yeah," I said, "I know, being nice, huh?"

Chrystal said, "Yeah, that's what I thought. So he asked me how many kids I had in the day care. He was following me to my car now, okay, telling me that he likes to see young women working and taking care of theirs."

"So what did you do when he started following you to your car with the kids?"

"Well, after I put my son in the car seat, he tried to kiss me as I raised my head from the backseat and got ready to get in the front seat. He said, 'I'd sure like to take you out!'"

"What did you do, girl?"

Chrystal said, "Aunt Bella, I couldn't do anything. I was scared, and he's a minster."

"Did you say anything to him?"

"No, I was scared. I told you."

"Well, I want his number, because he's not going to do this to you and think it's okay. Does Mama know what he has done?"

"No, I didn't tell Granny what happened yet."

"Well, let me be the one, okay?"

Chrystal didn't object. "If you want to, but she loves her pastor."

I hung up with Chrystal and thought about this man who called himself a man of God. The North Side was a very popular black church in the country where black people were migrating in the early eighties. I had met him on one of my visits when I was home and again at Mama's seventieth birthday party. I didn't like him then, and I knew why now.

"Hello." It was Mama on the other end of the receiver.

"I just finished talking to Ruth."

"You did?" I asked, knowing what she was about to tell me. "What's wrong, Mama?"

Mama started by saying, "Now don't get upset."

"Mama, what happened?"

"My pastor just asked my granddaughter out on a date."

"What! Lord have mercy."

"He told me he didn't know that she was part of my family."

"Mama, please," I said. "It could have been any loved one. He has no business talking to those young single mothers like that."

"I know." Mama sighed. "He was wrong, but he's only human. God tests us all."

I told Mama, "That was no test from God. He would like you to believe that, but I don't." I told Mama before she died that he was a wolf in sheep's clothing.

There he stood in all his filth with his rotten soul. "Let us all bow our heads and pray." I couldn't move my neck to bend it. I was fixated on his face. I sat there and stared at him so hard that he became transparent to me. Aunt Beverly took the floor, and I shifted my attention as she started to sing "His Eye Is on the Sparrow," my mama's favorite gospel song. She got a little full in the end, but she carried the song to its glory, with my aunt Cookie crying out, "Sister, my sister!" Beverly went back to her seat, and she let the tears flow. I could hear her sobs, along with a few others.

My focus was brought back to the pastor as he began to tell of my mama's time here on this earth, how she spent her last days being a brave and good soldier of the Lord, and how he had given her an award for the mother of the year.

My mama never failed to pay her church dues—the 10 percent that's due to God. It was becoming a pitch for paying your 10 percent. He stated that paying was a way to get your name on the appointment list, because everybody had an appointment with death. It was sounding more like a sermon. Cicely started to run up and down the aisle, as if she had the Holy Ghost, and yelled, "Preach, Pastor!" Tony tried to grab her arm, but she pulled away for one more turn halfway down the aisle.

The pastor then asked the members of his church to stand up—Why? I didn't really know. But he reminded them that one day they would be where my mother was and that if they have robbed God of what was his due, then their names would be on that appointment list too. The oldest of Mama's grandchildren were asked to come up and speak. Zoe spoke of Mama and what it was like to have a grandmother who would do anything for her family and how much she loved them. Zoe was struggling to find more words of compassion. She shouted out with tears running down her face, "Granny, I love you! You were the best granny anyone could ask for." Michelle, Maya's oldest daughter, held to the fact that her granny had been a wonderful grandmother and that she was proud that she had gotten to see her children before she had passed. Mama had more great-grandchildren than she had grandchildren. And for that she would live on in each of us.

My nephews Todd and Seth were the last to address the mourners. Seth was tearful when he took the mic from Michelle. He looked at each of us sitting in the front row, and then he spoke while looking at his mother, Cicely. "My granny was always there for my mama," he said. "She always had a meal for whoever came by. She never turned anyone away." With tears streaming down his face, he said he wished he had more time. "Granny, I miss you."

Todd first thanked his wife for her support during this time of sorrow and said that the trip from Atlanta was stressful on his family but that they were determined to make it. He was grateful for all his friends who had come out, as well. In closing he asked everyone to please join the family after the burial. Todd lacked something to be desired. He never mentioned his grandmother. I felt that what he took for confidence was his arrogance, like his father.

The pastor asked if there was anyone who had any remarks about Mama. The pastor from Burning Bush made note of the wonderful conversation they had when he had gone to visit her in the nursing home. It came time to view the body.

As the pastor came down from the pulpit to acknowledge the family, he finally made eyes contact. As he bent down to take my hand, I moved it and told him, "Get away from me!"

The mourners passed the coffin to view Mama for the last time. They embraced us with hugs and tears of sadness for our loss. The call came for the pallbearers to rise, and as Mama's casket was closed, we were all given a white angel that sat on the four corners of her coffin. We walked behind Mama as they carried her out to the hearse. Zoe, Danielle, Cholet, and the kids all gathered around me before I got into the limo.

"We want to hug you, Mama, before you get to the cemetery," Zoe said. We group hugged, something Danielle didn't like to do but did without objection. "We got you an obituary, Ma, if you didn't get one."

"Okay, I hadn't gotten one," I told her.

I waited to see Aunt Kat to thank her for coming and being there for our family. She said she'd see me later. I didn't want to watch as they put Mama in the hearse. I opened the door to the limo, and Edward was already sitting inside, with his face drenched in tears. I reached into my purse and gave him a Kleenex to wipe his face.

"Bella, I don't have anybody. What am I going to do without Mama around? I can't even go to the house. We've got nothing left, sis."

"Edward," I said, "look at me. We still have memories."

"You need to be strong for your daughters. They were looking for you."

"Have you talked to them?" I asked him.

"No. I just came and got into the car."

Tony opened the door next and climbed in, followed by Philip. Edward and I stopped talking when the others got in the limo. The funeral director was running around, putting stickers on the windshields of everyone's car as he told which car to pull behind which car. We slowly pulled from the curb behind the hearse. I took Maya's hand in mine and held it. She was unresponsive. She slowly pulled her hand away.

We started the slow ride to Mama's final resting place. I looked at my watch. It was a little before twelve. That was a good omen. I made a wish in my heart and thanked the light and dark that gave me the strength. As the funeral procession pulled around the corner, I could see the line of cars as we drove through the cemetery gate. There were more cars than I could count as we turned each small corner, winding our way to the spot where Maya and I had been two days earlier. There was a tent, and a huge hole had been dug. Cars stretched out behind us as they all came to a stop. We waited as the coffin was placed over the hole and flowers draped over her casket.

My heart was gripped with grief, and my soul was low in the moment. When the car door opened, I wanted to take Maya's hand, but I dared not touch it again. We all started down the small hill toward the tree where Mama waited to be placed in mother earth. Everyone was making their way to the tent. As I looked around I could see my girls with their children, making their way to stand behind me. The pastor said a few words I would recall later. He stared me down as he spoke. "The light shines on the good, as well as the bad." Raising his hands toward the sky, he said, "Notice the sun shines on us here today. And even sinners can be forgiven."

As I sat there, the tears that I had fought so hard to hold back came forward like a warm stream running down my face. Teardrops were falling from my chin. I said in repentance, "Forgive yourself." There was no emotion, just the flowing of my tears now. *I will remember this day: December 8.* The years wouldn't matter.

This day of all days marked a moment that my life changed forever, like when you get married or have children or grandchildren—those moments. Those days become marked in your memory. Joy and sadness had come to an agreement. I had to love with what was left.

When my children grew up and left home, and I could no longer be the goodwill, I learned to wish them well and my love would flow. The home magically transformed back into a home for holidays, cookouts, and family occasions.

Divorce destroys everything in its path and becomes one of life's greatest lessons. Take stock now, and put this moment in order. "Yes! God made the sun!"

Cholet brought me a rose from the casket and handed it to me. "Mama, I'm not going back to the church."

"Why?" I asked.

"The kids have been up all day, and the baby needs a nap. We are going home, and I'll bring them to the hotel for breakfast and a swim tomorrow."

"Okay, sweetheart, that will be fine. I'll order room service at about ten. How's that?"

"Mommy," Danielle broke into the conversation, "are you going back to the church?"

"I guess I should." I had to make a decision. *Should I? Should I get back into the limo?* I didn't want to, but I had to. I wanted to see it to the end.

So I did go back to the church. I climbed the hill and got back into the limo. Everyone was there but Cicely. She came up the hill carrying an armful of flowers. Edward got my attention. "Sis, Uncle Brother isn't looking too good,"

"No, he doesn't. Mama had told me the last time he came to the nursing home that he couldn't remember from one minute to the next what she was talking about. She asked Aunt Eldora if he had been to see a doctor." With a smile I knew how that conversation had really gone. I knew Mama was still questioning her sister-in-law.

"Yeah, that was Mama all right," Edward said.

We settled in for the ride back to the church. We went through the side entrance of the church and down some basement stairs that turned into a long hall. The dining hall was full of people eating and socializing. I didn't know where my girls were. I didn't see Zoe or Danielle. I turned and went into the ladies room.

"Bella," Aunt Beverly called me after I had washed my hands and was leaving, "I need to ask you something. Did you and your sister Cicely get into it at Reese's house when you came into town?"

"Aunt Beverly, it doesn't matter what you heard. You know how Cicely is. I don't want to talk about it."

On my way back to the dining hall, friends were giving their condolences. I would have loved to stop and say a few words. There were no words. I looked around the dining hall to get my bearings. I saw Aunt Ellie in white, sitting at what was the immediate-family table. I started over toward her and saw Cicely and Maya whispering to each other. They had been doing this a lot. I turned and went to the line. The hall was full and noisy, with people talking and moving about. I still hadn't seen my girls.

Standing there in line, I noticed my niece Michelle sitting in front of the head table, trying to calm this baby she was holding on her lap. "Hi, Michelle." It was the first time I had seen her since she sold her business and moved to Atlanta to work for Seth.

"Oh, hi, Aunt Bella. I meant to say something to you standing in the church earlier."

"That's fine, honey. Whose baby are you holding?"

"This is my baby."

"How old is he?"

"Oh, he is going on two."

I looked over at Maya, puzzled that she hadn't told me. My niece had a baby, and I knew nothing about it.

"You don't have to stand in line. You're Sister Cicely Colman's sister, right?" The voice came from behind me. It was a church member. A short, round, light-skinned lady with fiery red hair took me by my arm and broke into our conversation.

"Aunt, I'll see you at Aunt Cicely's house later tonight."

"Okay, sweetheart," I told her.

The menu was fried chicken corn and mashed potatoes with dinner rolls. I took my plate and looked over at my sisters and brothers sitting there. I could feel eyes watching me as I was stood there watching my siblings. A strong energy was coming from the table where my aunts Carmen, Beverly, and Lillie were sitting. I made my way over to the table, and they made room for me. I sat the plate down in front of me and never touched the food.

"Now, Bella, tell me," Aunt Carmen said. "Did your sisters give all of Reese's things away when she went into the nursing home or after she died?"

"I don't know, Aunt Carmen." I didn't have the answer to many questions.

"You know why your girls didn't come back to the church, right?"

"No, I was looking for them."

"Bella, it's a damn shame what they are doing, but you be strong. They are more upset with you because you are going to be okay. They are going to have it really hard with your mama gone. The bad might outweigh the good now, but the wind does change. Honey, we know what went on at the house before the wake."

"Huh?"

"Cicely is a mess."

I sat there listening to my aunts fill me in on their many visits to the house and the manner in which Cicely was talking to their sister, calling her an old mean lady. "Shut your mouth. You're old." These were the words they were using now. Aunt Charlotte stated that she stopped coming when she asked Cicely to take Mama to the store, because she couldn't make it by. Cicely told her no because she had made plans, and Aunt Charlotte shouldn't tell her sister she was going to do something and not do it. Charlotte said, "Many times Cicely left your mama walking to the bus stop when Cicely could have given her a ride to work."

"Please," Aunt Carmen chimed in. "You remember on one of your visits home, when I came by the house to see your mama and you?"

"Yes," I said. "I was going to pick up takeout. I left Cicely, you, and Mama in the kitchen. When I returned, you told me they had to rush Mama to the hospital."

"Yeah, and what do you think happened that afternoon? Your sister talked to your mother so badly after you left."

I got up from the table without a word. I had heard enough. I knew they wanted to have a relationship with Mama, and Cicely had made that impossible for most. Danielle had called me almost every other day about how she would help take care of Mama, but Cicely would ask her to leave because she was going out. She said that Tony would be there for Mama. But Danielle had her CNA license. The day came when Cicely told me she couldn't do it anymore. I asked Cicely to please wait until I got there. I would help her with Mama. Mama had been home just less than a week. I was away with James, my husband.

I walked around spending time talking with my uncles. I invited them to come to New York. Edward came over to me. "Sis, come on. The limo is waiting to take us back to the house."

"Okay, here I come."

Uncle Brother promised to call me. I kissed him on his cheek and hugged him around his neck. I knew it would be the last time I saw him alive. I could sense death's presence when it was near. It came to me in dreams or shadows. I didn't see Mama's death door open. I believe she opened it and made the decision to leave. But my uncle's door in my dream was open. However, he was not alone when he went through it. I had always confided in Mama about my dreams. I had seen death take members of the family from the situations that played out like a movie.

I waved good-bye to Mrs. Parks and her family. LeAnn didn't come to Mama's funeral. She explained to me the night of the wake how she didn't even go to her own mother's funeral. The family got together and took care of LeAnn's mama until she passed in her own bed. I admired them for that. It was something we couldn't do as a family. I understood now, as memories of growing up showed me that it wasn't the material things of life but quality by which LeAnn and her family demonstrated when they cared for their dying mother. There was a sentimental past.

Mama would say, "I don't want you with those girls across the street from Papa's neighborhood grocery store." It wasn't until my aunt Ellie told Mama that she knew their mother that it was okay to play with them. LeAnn would come and sit with me on my front stairs when I had to babysit my brothers.

I gathered my thoughts and made my way back up the stairs into the evening wind. It was getting late. Edward met me at the limo. Maya and Carl were already in the car. Tony was saying his good-byes to a couple of his high school buddies. I was taking the third and final ride, to end up where it began.

The limo pulled up to the house. Once again I asked myself why I didn't leave the burial with Danielle and Zoe. More so, why had I come back to Mama's house? But I knew now that I had the strength. I wanted to face the last time I would be together with my sisters and brothers. This was heart wrenching.

There were a hundred names for how I was feeling. My spirit had been faithful throughout this devastating time. I knew what I was up against, and my siblings knew how I felt. We all went inside. Maya and Cicely went straight to Mama's bedroom. I was close behind. Maya shut the bedroom door before I could reach the kitchen. I walked back into the living room and sat on the sofa. The house was busy with Cicely's sons, their wives, and the grandchildren. I looked around at all the figurines I had bought over the years. I wanted those things. I thought, *Take them all now! Who cares what they think. Take them all!* There were many things that I had gotten Mama that I wanted. I got up and walked out into the entrance hall. The portrait of me sat on a shelf, along with a portrait of Maya and Cicely. I had given it to Mama. *Take it!* I wanted that back too.

I went into the room that used to be Zoe's bedroom, before Cicely moved into it. The room was empty now, except for Mama's computer and a chair. I sat alone in the chair. The kids came and went, running through the house. Maya came from the bedroom and into the room where I was sitting and said, "Cicely doesn't want to be bothered. She's lying down. And I'm going home."

## Closing Chapter

The damage had been done. They were making it known to me that the boundary had been set and I was not to cross it. I was mourning the death of more than a parent, but also my sisters. The doorbell rang. I got up to answer it, and there were my daughters! "Mommy, are you ready to come with us now?"

"Yes, I'm ready to go home." It was over now, and there was no going back. What had been done or said could not be undone. But I wasn't done yet.

On the ride back to Danielle's house, the girls talked about the legal options that my brothers and I had concerning Mama's estate. I knew that I didn't want to talk about that yet. What I wanted was the gifts I had given Mama over the years. I wanted to sit among my sisters and brothers and go through Mama's things together, recalling the memories from each item we went through. I wanted us to cry together and remember we were all we had now and to promise to hold our families together and to spend time with each other. We were a big family. All six of us were grandparents. We needed to close the circle around us. These were the things I wanted.

"Mommy," Danielle called, "what are you thinking?"

"I guess I was wishing something that might be hopeless and far from where we are now."

"What, Mommy? You want to be a family? You got your family, Mommy. Family is love, Mommy, and your sisters and your brothers need to learn the meaning of that word before they can move into any kind of love for the family. They are selfish, and you witnessed that these three days you were here."

Zoe looked over at me sitting in the front seat. She took my hand and said, "I'm sorry that you don't have the kind of family that you think you should, but you will always have your children who love you unconditionally, and for now that has to be enough."

Danielle put her hand on my shoulder and told me, "Mommy, I do have some good news for you. Cholet said she was leaving Tiburon and taking the kids back to New York with you when you leave."

I sighed, relieved that Cholet no longer was going to let herself be a punching bag. I called Cholet the minute we were back at the hotel. Philip was there, packed and waiting for us. "Hey, everybody, did you have a nice time at Mama's?"

"No, we didn't go to Granny's house," Zoe said. "We went and got Mama. Where was your family, Uncle Philip?"

"Shit, you didn't think I was going back to Mama's after all that stuff went down. I stayed with my daughter and my grandkids. You know, Bella," he went on to say, "Mama was the reason a lot of this happened the way it did."

We checked out and headed for the car. Cholet said she would be staying at her girlfriend's that night and to pick her up there because she didn't want Tiburon to know she was leaving him. Just knowing that made the trip worthwhile. I was grateful Philip had decided to stay at Lorna's house after we left the hotel, so he dropped us at Danielle's house, and he headed for Lorna's. Philip and Lorna were high school sweethearts. They had three daughters together and several grandchildren, whom he hadn't seen since he moved to New York.

I poured myself a glass of wine the minute we got inside the door. I sat at the kitchen table, wondering if the person I had been before was going to ever show up. I had changed. I would never be that person again. I didn't know what tomorrow would bring, but I was assured of one thing. I had given my mother her flowers while she was living. For that reason I had no regrets.

We started for home bright and early the next morning; I hadn't talked to my sisters after last night. I didn't mention anything more about Mama's will. The morning sun was warm, and the sky was blue and clear. We picked up Cholet at her girlfriend's house and made our way to the airport. I missed James, but I was happy that he didn't attend. I had told him it was okay not to come because of the drama. I was on my way back to the arms that I longed so much to have hold me.

The company of my grandchildren made my heart sigh, and my soul was full of joy. This was bliss! Few find it. I had, and my heart was wrapped around it for now. I learned that it is all fleeting. You must feel it and hold it for as long as you can.

The flight was restful, and the kids slept through the nonstop flight. The car pulled into the driveway late in the night. James had picked us up from the airport. "Come on, everybody. We're here!" Tate yelled.

I helped Cholet with the baby. Philip took his suitcase from the trunk and put it in the trunk of his car he had left in the driveway. "Look, sis, I'm not coming in. It's late, and I need to get home. I go to work tomorrow, okay?"

I gave Philip a kiss good-bye and went into the house. James was busy with Drew and Joy. Zoe took her suitcase upstairs. I was too tired to take a shower. I fell into the bed and later rolled into James's arms and fell asleep.

The next day the phone rang. It was Cicely. "Hi, sis, how are you doing?"

"I'm good, Cicely. I wasn't looking for you to call me."

"Bella, I'm sorry for the way I treated you, but I was only following our big sister's wishes. Maya didn't want to meet, so I wanted to do what she wanted me to do."

"So, Cicely," I said, "you would have fought me because Maya felt she didn't want to talk with her sisters and brothers about their mother's will." I didn't hold back now.

Cicely opened that door of opportunity, and I wasn't going to let it close. I expressed how hateful they were and that I received nothing of what I had given Mama.

"I know," Cicely said, "but Maya wanted Mama's jewelry. I saved the dove necklace you bought her. I have it for you if you want."

"Yes, I want it."

"Can you forgive me?"

"Cicely, there isn't anything that you could do that I wouldn't forgive you for."

"I'm sorry," she kept saying. Then she asked if Zoe was home.

"No, she's at work. Why?"

"Well, the funeral home secretary needs to talk to her."

"Why?" I asked.

"I don't know, but she is going to call her, okay?"

"Sure, Cicely." I hung up the phone, called Danielle, and told her Cicely had called and apologized for what happened.

"Ma," Danielle said, "what do you really think that was all about? It seems to me that if Maya put her up to do the things she did when you were there, then what is she apologizing for if she felt she was right? You should have told her to put you on a three-way with Maya and then ask for forgiveness, if she really meant it. I know there's more to it."

"She said she was giving me the necklace I bought Mama."

"Ma! What about all the other things? The bracelet—did you tell her you wanted that back from Aunt Ellie?"

"No, Danielle, I didn't." I told Danielle that she also called to tell me that the funeral home secretary wanted to talk with Zoe."

"Zoe!" Danielle said, surprised.

"Yeah, I guess we won't know until Zoe speaks to her."

"Well, have Zoe call me after she talks to them," Danielle said.

"Okay, honey, I'll tell her to call you." I hung up the phone and wanted to call Maya and tell her everything that Cicely had said. I picked up the telephone and dialed the number. I thought better and hung up the phone before the first ring. I hated both my sisters for their trickery. The rage inside me screamed. I needed to find another way to feel.

Later that evening the phone call from the funeral home came. "Hello."

"May I please speak with Zoe?"

I called her to the phone. Zoe kept saying she didn't understand why she was calling her. After she got off the phone, she told me that she needed her to sign over a policy that Mama had left to her.

"What? Why would you have to sign over your policy?"

Zoe had no idea that Mama had bequeathed everything to her. There was nothing mentioned in the will. The will stated that all of her assets would be divided equally among her children. The lady from the funeral home explained to Zoe that the family needed her to sign over the policy to cover the final costs for mama's funeral. Cicely's telephone call was never about me and her, nor did it have anything to do with her being sorry. It was another ploy, with Maya once again working in the background.

What bitches they were! Anger rose up in me again. How many of those policies in that shopping bag Maya had belonged to other members of the family? They had the nerve to want me to sign mine over. They didn't call the secretary. Hell no! It was not over. The next chapter was being written. What more could they do to hurt me? I told Zoe to do what her heart led her to do.

This was another struggle—to rise above and see again with the eye of God. I contacted a lawyer through the Per Legal, of which I had become a member. I could have taken them through the drama of a probate court, but I decided—unlike my mama, who took her sisters to court—to let karma deal with them. If anything, hope guided me. I had the lawyers draw up a letter so that Maya must disclose all the information concerning Mama's will. They never responded. Zoe later called Michelle, Maya's oldest daughter, since Maya wouldn't return her call.

After the funeral, it was about a month before Tony called to say Cicely had asked him and Aunt Rose's son, who was staying at my mama's house, to leave, and she wanted the house to herself. So her son Todd advised her to put them out. We had talked about a headstone for Mama, but Cicely never called. I told Tony to come to New York and live with me. We started to make arrangements to purchase a headstone for Mama's grave. I called my sisters and my brothers who were home in Louisiana if they all wanted to donate. No one called me back but Edward. In the end, Zoe, Edward, Tony, and I saw to it that Mama had a headstone.

Three months after Mama died, her oldest brother, Paul Jr., passed. Six months later my mama's brother Uncle Wilbert passed way. And then in January 2008, Mama's grandson Anthony Jr. died. Three family members followed Mama in death, as if she had called them. I know my uncles missed their sister dearly and went to keep her company. At least that is the way I chose to see it. I once again had to make the trip to Louisiana. This time I did not see my sister Maya until the day of Anthony Jr.'s funeral. Cicely and I spoke over the phone, but not much was said at the funeral.

But there we were, brought together again. I took in the grief of another death. The wounds of pain and sorrow from Mama's death had not yet healed. They became infested. I greeted my sisters with kisses. I embraced them as you would friends. Cicely started to cry and said, "Sister, I love you."

Zoe, who came with me, got up and went outside to wait in the car. I made it through the wake and funeral with minimal communication with my sister Maya.

Later at the burial, after we had all marched down to the grave site, Anthony was buried next to his son. Philip and Cicely noticed that there was a headstone for Mama. Philip fell to the ground. "Mama! That's my mama lying there!"

Cicely did a U-turn back up the little hill to tell Maya, who didn't or couldn't walk down, there was a headstone.

Yes, we had purchased Mama's headstone without their financial help. Thank God we did. I stood there looking at Anthony's casket, and I looked over at Mama's gravestone.

Mama's death was now a closed chapter. My nephew died a year after Mama, and so did two of her brothers. Soon to follow would be my brother Anthony and my sister Cicely. They would die within two months of each other.

They would rest next to Mama. I knew Mama's last wishes. I knew Mama's spirit had called to them. Softly I spoke as the tip of my tongue tasted a tear that had rolled down my cheek. "Mama, are you now at peace?"

## The End